# Finger Painting

"Techniques of oil painting"

Shyam Das Dr. Mamta

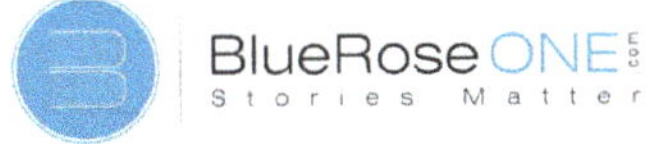

BLUEROSE PUBLISHERS
India | U.K.



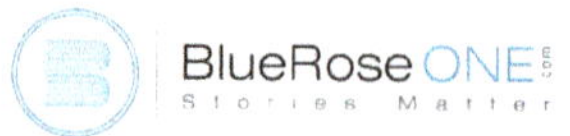


For permissions requests or inquiries regarding this publication, please contact:

BLUEROSE PUBLISHERS
www.BlueRoseONE.com
info@bluerosepublishers.com
+91 8882 898 898
+4407342408967

ISBN: 978-93-5628-357-2

Cover design: Aveek
Typesetting: Rohit

First Edition: July 2023

*This book is about finger painting. This is a fast technique mainly used in oil painting. Technique used in this type of painting is just opposite to the normal oil painting. Time taken to complete one painting is 10-15 minutes only. This book intends to encourage people who are not expert painters but are interested in learning oil painting.*

**DEDICATED TO OUR PARENTS**

LATE SRI DAMODAR DAS

LATE SMT RADHA DEVI

AND

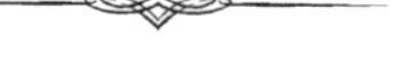

**THANKS TO**

ABHINAV RAJ

RAVI RANJAN

ANURAG RANJAN

RAJAT

SATYJEET BHAGAT

**THANKS TO**

ALL THOSE WHOSE LOVE AND BLESSINGS WERE ALWAYS WITH US.

THANK GOD FOR ALL YOUR BLESSINGS.

# About the Author

The Author of this book, *Shyam Das*, is a born artist. He has done his schooling from Notre Dame Academy, Munger, Jamalpur, Bihar. Painting has been his passion since his childhood. His first Guru was his school teacher who taught about the techniques used in drawings. He is Graduate in English Honors from R&DJ college, Munger. He holds a senior diploma in Fine Arts from Bangia University (West Bengal) which is a branch of RavindraBharti University. He holds many awards. He belongs to a place in Bihar called Munger. He runs a painting and music institute at his home town, Munger. He held many art exhibitions at New Delhi and solo exhibitions at Mumbai. He was recognized as a proponent of finger painting on several TV channels. (IBN7 cannel on 10th October, 2008).

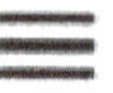
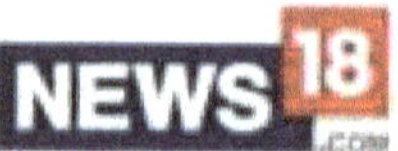

# Meet Shyam Das, a proponent of finger-painting

**First published:** April 10, 2008, 7:30 PM IST | **Updated:** April 10, 2008

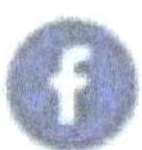
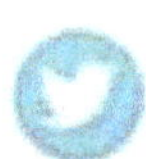
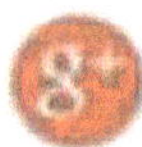
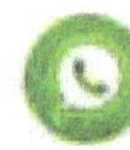

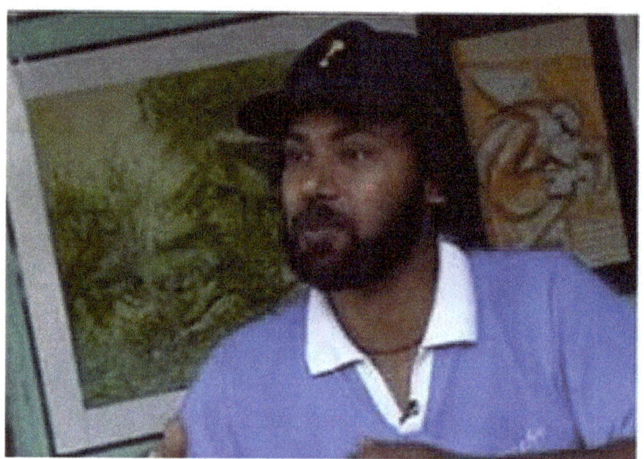

# About the co-author

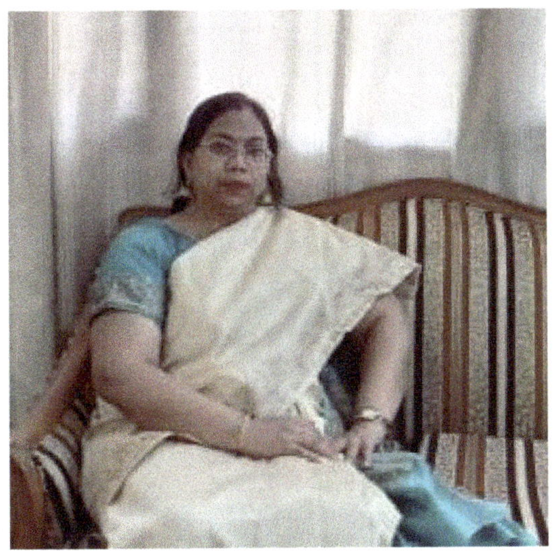

*Dr. Mamta*

Dr. Mamta is a Senior Assistant Professor in the department of Linguistics, University of Delhi, Delhi. She has done her Ph.D from Jawaharlal Nehru University (JNU), New Delhi in Linguistics. She has done her schooling from Notre Dame Academy, Munger, Jamalpur, Bihar. Her home town is Munger,Bihar. She is a NET holder and has been awarded by CIIL Scholarship, Mysore. She works in the field of Language disorder and learning disorder like Dyslexia and has been working with children with dyslexia. Paintings and music connects with such children and helps to deal easily with them. It helps in creating a bond.

# Contents

# Oil Finger Painting and its Style

Finger Painting described in this book is about the newly developed style of oil Painting which is unique in itself.

Before I describe about this newly developed style of Painting style, I would like to describe about the style of Painting from the primitive age of oil painting.

Oil Painting in primitive age was a very slow and steady form of painting. Inoil painting the process begins from the base of the subject. It is done layer by layer. For example- the darkest colour in the painting is used first and slowly it moves towards the light colour.The process is very old and it still continues today. Several Artists have tried to increase the speed of painting by their own intelligence by using certain technique such as dash and swagar by john constable and many others. I will describe the stage of painting of various Artists from 18th century till now in further paragraph to understand the style and development in oil Painting.

For the Finger Painting in oil colour I have discovered a technique which is completely a unique technique from the old slow and steadymethod to fast method.

Oil colour is usually used by brush. Different types of brushes are used in oil Painting. Not only brushes are used but different types of spatulas are also used.

To create a unique effect in painting soft cotton cloths are also used. I will also describe in further paragraph how the old masters or painters used certain things instead of brush to give a new look and new strokes. But still the process was the same as I described earlier from dark to light shade. First the dark colour was used and dried in sunlight and then the strokes of light colour were done on it. But in the newly developed style of Painting which is known as oil Finger Painting style is different from the old style of oil painting.

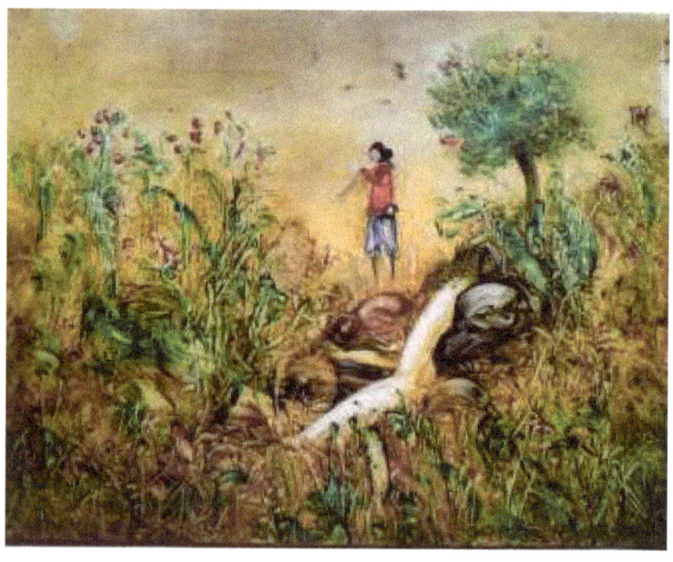

In this technique the shade, light and the entire stroke used is at the same time. There is no layer by layer painting. There is no drying system of one coating of painting first and then start with another coating. There is no dark to light process. The process is as fast as water colour. The technique is highly useful to create a new design or image. This technique is not necessarily be used by the Artists or the people who is concerned about this but this technique can be used by those people also who are not experts but has love for Art irrespective of whether they know about painting or not.

This is only one coat painting like in water colour. All the shades and light will be done in only one coat. The use of brush is not at all necessary in this technique. The strokes are done by the finger tips and the nails. This is the fastest way of oil painting till the date. The movement of the finger will keep on creating the strokes. The most relevant thing in this technique is that the painting can be finished in one coat. Till now there is no technique to finish the painting in one coat with all together effect of light and shade but this technique can do so. The strokes which will take five to six days to give its effect in old and primitive style, the new style of painting will take five to ten minutes in this technique.

The slow and steady style of painting as well as one by one coating costs lots of time and money. There is a need for new technique which can save both time and money. Therefore, my technique fulfils this great demand. This technique is more than even water colour, crayons, pencil colour and all the other medium of colours. This is a revolution in the field of oil painting and a beginning of new era of oil painting. We can also say that there is a change of oil painting era.

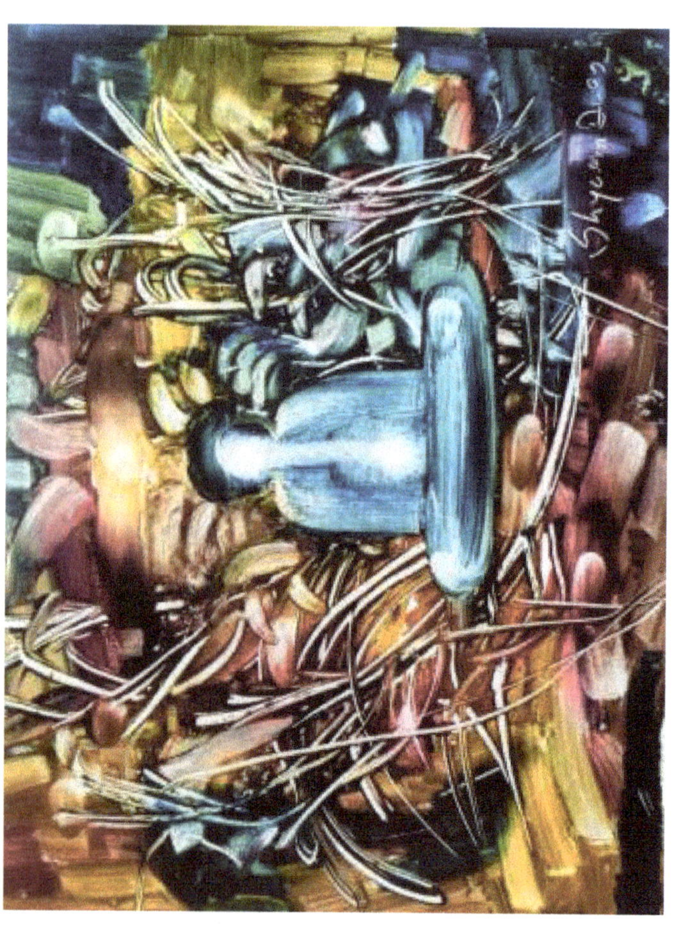

# Materials used in finger oil painting

This finger painting is a highly developed and new technique. In this technique, the colour is used with linseed oil. The colour should be mixed with the finger on the paper or canvas itself.

## Preparing the canvas for painting

The canvas should be smooth and slippery. If the canvas is rough or not so smooth, the strokes won't be clean and distinct. For this purpose rub the canvas with a sand paper and coat with white (flake, or titanium) oil colour at least two times. The first coat should be heavy. After drying the first coat properly put the second coat properly by brush and using turpentine oil. After drying it in sunlight or by dryer, again rub the canvas or paper properly with sand paper. The more slippery the canvas would be, the more effective will be the strokes.

If you want to paint on paper, the process is very easy. First of all, coat the paper with any enamel colour using brush. Let it dry for at least one day. If you can dry it in sunlight, it is better or you can dry the paper by dryer.

After drying it properly, for better result, put a coat of white oil colour using linseed oil and a little bit of turpentine oil. The colour used in finger oil painting can be of any quality. For e.g. oil colour tube for student or oil colour for artists.

The oil used in this process is linseed oil only. Linseed oil should be sprayed on the paper or canvas before painting.

It can be evenly sprayed with the help of rags of clothes or by any type of flat brush. While using the oil on paper or canvas, keep the paper or canvas straight on the floor or on any table you would like to paint on. The canvas or paper should be flat on the table. If you put it on an easel or stand, the oil will slide down. It is very important to keep the canvas or paper flat on table or on floor when you start painting. Keep the canvas flat on the table and see that the surface is not irregular anywhere. If it is up or down anywhere, the oil will seep that side and the painting will not be as good as you imagined it to be. Some rags of clothes or cotton will be used at the time when the colour or oil accumulates anywhere. You can tap the cotton on it to make it balanced as your desire to get the effect. You can also use some type of thin sticks or match sticks to have astraight line stroke or curve line stroke in the painting.

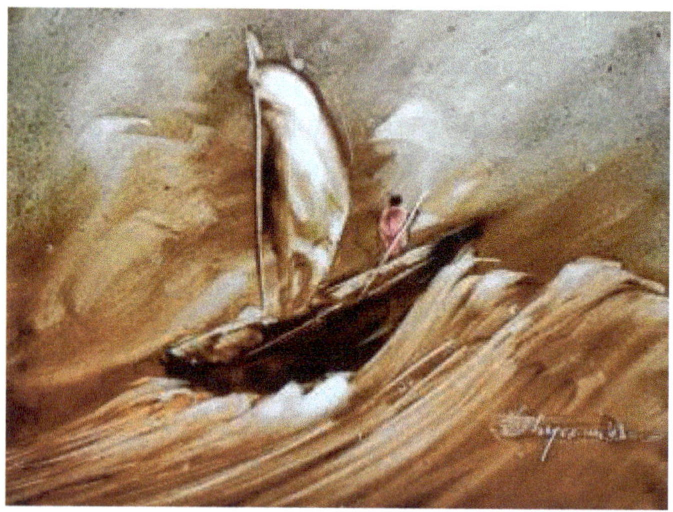

The last material used in oil finger painting is dry clothes. This is used to erase where the colour or oil is more than required.

Turpentine oil is used in this technique in a balanced manner. Use it where it is needed more or use less according to the need of the type of painting. It can be light or dark shade required in the painting. For example- where the colour needs to be light, take a piece of cotton or any foam for buffering the painting and make the required area light as you wish it to be.

In some paintings, where the colour needs to be very dark, the colour should be taken out directly from the tube itself.

Using linseed oil can be done by two methods. The first method is to take the linseed oil by some piece of cloth or by any type of flat brush and spray it evenly. The second method is to put the paper or canvas flat on the ground and pour the linseed oil from the bottle on it carelessly. When oil is poured on it, lift the canvas and straighten it so the oil spreads everywhere. Put lots of linseed oil and straighten it so the oil on the canvas is spread evenly and keep a tray or something of plastic so when the oil is dropped in it so that the rest of the oil can be used for later.

These were the material used in this process. Further I will explain the use of colour and the types of strokes you wish to create and the painting.

Every painting has new and creative strokes on it. It is explained separately for differentpaintings. For learning the technique properly, it is advised to practice the method on paper first. The quality of paper should be thick, smooth and gloss.

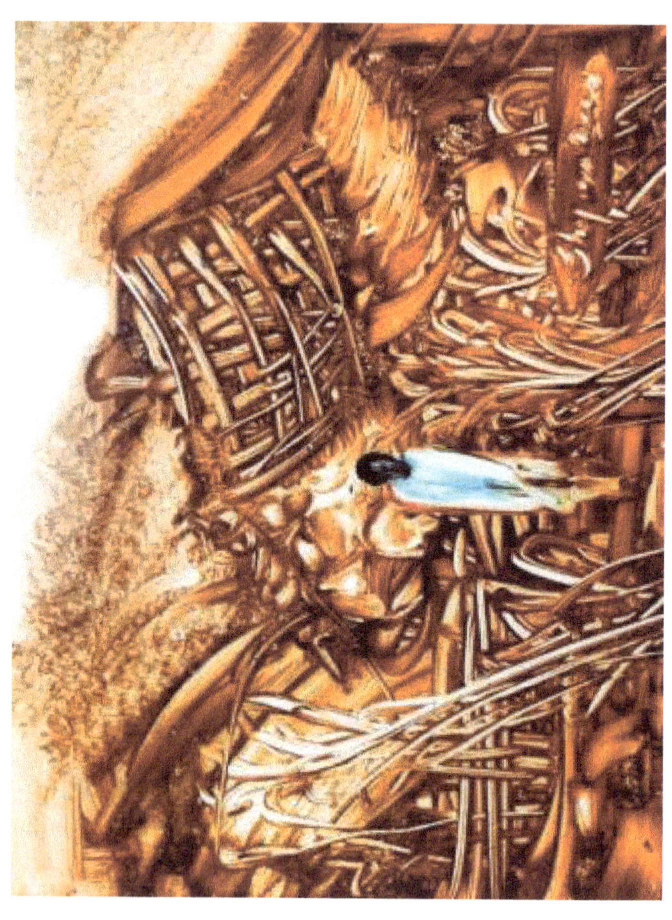

## To practice on paper, the following steps are required to create a good art work:-

**Step 1** - Select the size of paper you want to make and coat the paper evenly using enamel colour.

**Step 2** – The coat of enamel should be thin in the first coat. Dry it for at least six hour.

**Step 3**- Touch the paper by finger to check if the paper is not sticky

**Step 4**- When the paper is dry put a coat of white oil colour using turpentine oil on it. The coat should be thick and evenly painted with a flat brush.

Now the paper for finger oil painting is ready. You can start painting on it as you wish with only your finger tips.

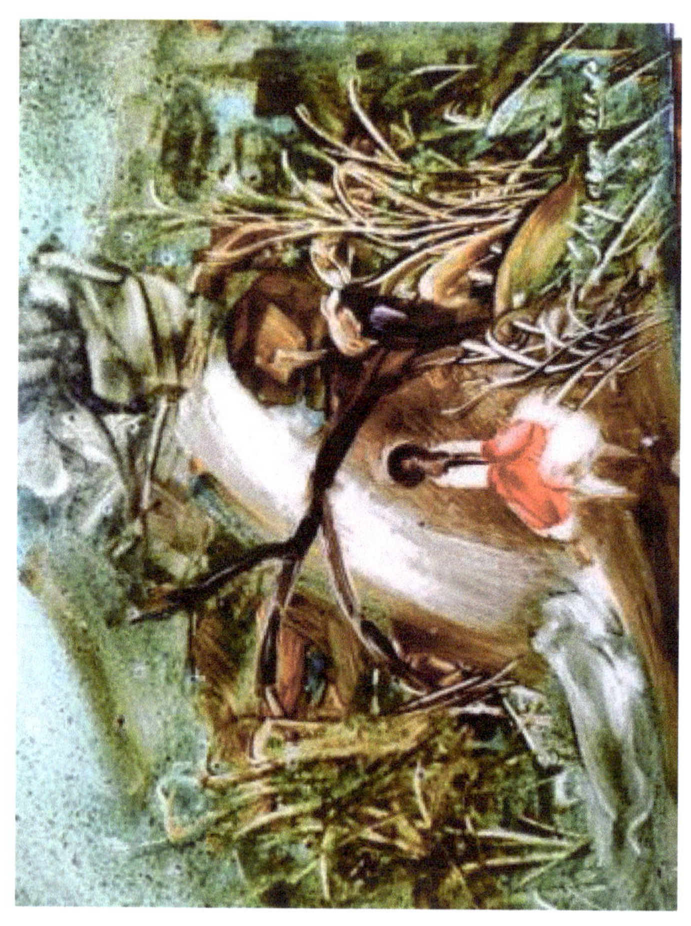

## Process of painting with your fingers

When your paper is ready, fix it on a painting board.

**Step 1** – Take a small piece of cloth and put it in the linseed oil and buff the paper evenly. Take care that the oil is evenly spread on the paper. For first trial take some colour and put it on the paper and rub it carelessly to create any type of image. Take colours directly from the oil colour tube to your fingertips and rub it.

**Step 2** - Now start creating strokes on the dark side of the painting. Use all your fingers as you desire. Put all your fingers on the painting and squeeze it. When you squeeze your fingers, numerous strokes will be created in the painting. The efficiency of strokes will depend on the quality of the paper or canvas. The more slippery the paper is, the more efficient will be the strokes.

**Step 3** – The final stage is highlighting. For highlights, press your finger tips on the desired area and make it slip where you want. At last, when you see that you need more highlights, you can use a piece of cotton and buff on the area to highlight it. If you want to change the colour anywhere, you can erase it with cotton and make it neat and clean and the area will become white. You can take your desired colour on your finger tip and rub it gently on it to give light and shade in the newly covered area. Perform the above mentioned process very gently.

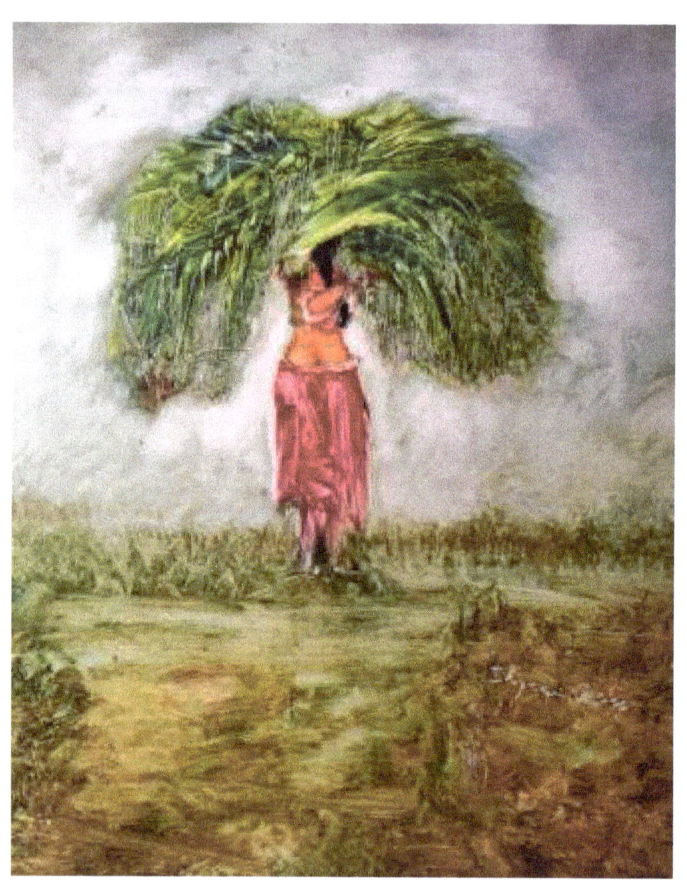

# How J discovered finger oil painting

Finger oil painting is a discovery in itself. There is an incident how I started painting only with finger. Once I made an oil painting on canvas for exhibition purpose and at the same time somebody cameasa buyer. The person was inspired by the painting but he had a small request to remove an object from that painting. This was an oil painting and to remove something from it needs time. He didn't have time he had only one hour in India. He was ready to go abroad.

To remove the object from the painting I used white enamel colour with my finger tips as this colour dries fast and removed the object with my fingertip so that I can give the painting to the buyer.

The buyer of this painting was inspired by the quick and fast work. He asked me how I did this so quickly. Then I toldhim about the whole thing that I did it with my finger. He said you paint better with fingers then by brush. If you practice painting only by finger you can do better. That moment was the beginning of finger painting but that was only in my mind. Gently I practiced it for a long time on paper as well as on canvas and from that time it became a new technique in the field of oil painting. Since then I started using this technique and painted several paintings which I will be sharing through this book.

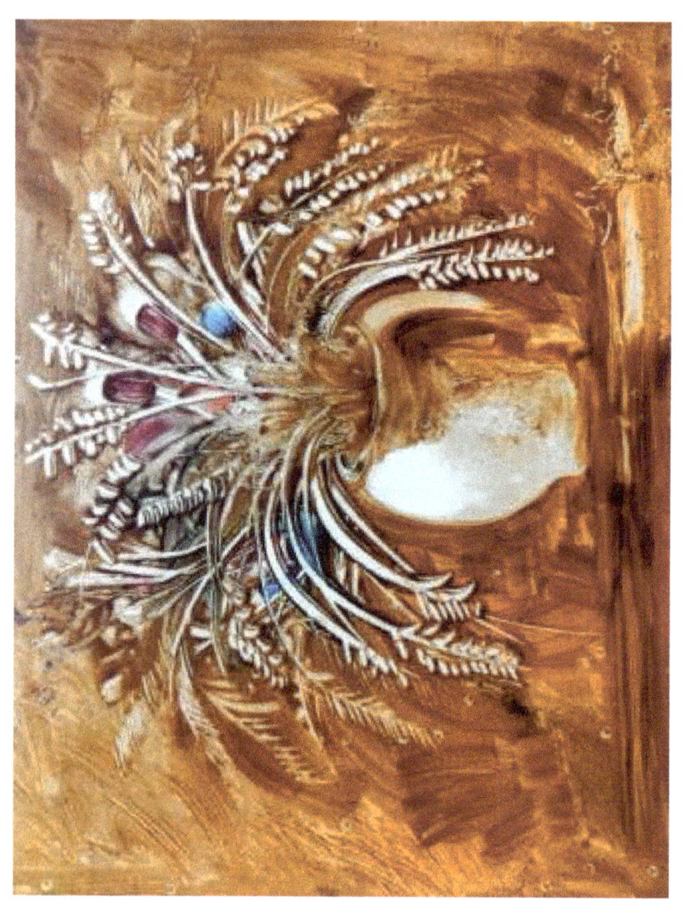

# History of the oil painting

Oil painting started around 7th century C.E. in Afghanistan. It was first of all introduced by some Buddhist artist. At that time the colour was mixed in oil and then it was used with the help of brush. After some time, around 15th century this technique was brought to Europe.

In India it is not known who introduced oil painting but some European who stayed in India started this trend of oil painting. Although it was not practiced at common places but was found inside the caves. In India it was found in Bhimbetka caves in Madhya Pradesh.

In Europe, the consistent pattern of art became clear only with the art of ancient Greece. Before 1800, the Christian church was the major centre of art. All the famous artist of Europe was commission to paint in the church. The subject was also religious. European art was arranged in a number of stylistic paintings. Broadly the period is classical by Zantine art, Goethe art, Neo classical art, Medieval art, Modern art, Post modernism art and New European art. In all types of art and paintings, brush was used to paint on the wall, caves or on the canvas. The colour was mixed in oil of walnut or poppies to produce the desired art work.

# Style variation in oil painting during $18^{th}$ century

In $18^{th}$ century oil painting was the most popular in Europe. Although it was practiced by certain great artists but the process of painting was the same slow and steady process. It was painted by the same process using brush, spatula and sometimes by certain special type of brush made by the artist himself. But some great masters tried to reform it by using their self- created tools other then the brush or spatula. In short I would like to describe about the prominent artist of $18^{th}$ century who tried their own techniques and methods.

L. David, the artist in the regime of Napoleon Bonaparte in France painted several Paintings of Napoleon and in the background of the painting he tried to give different type of strokes using small pieces of cloth. After the base coating was completed he used to put the strokes in the painting.

Vincent Van Gosh a very prominent artist of $18^{th}$ century was a realistic oil painting artist but he tried something new without using brush or spatula. He used to put the colour directly from the colour tube on the canvas. The colour on the canvas was over whelmed by the colour tube and no brush or anything was used to mix it or make it swift. In this type of painting, colour was used too much and drying was also time taking but this was a new reform in oil painting. Painting of Vincent Van Gosh is still today preserved in the museum and is also the most expensive painting of the world.

As compared to all those exclusive experiment in painting world, the finger painting keeps an exclusive value. In finger oil painting the colour used is very thin and the surface of canvas or paper is very smooth. To create a toning in this type of paintings, it does not needs drying or layer wise coating of colour. This process is opposite of the old traditional of oil painting process.

To create tones in the painting you need to balance the colour by the pressure of fingers. First the colour is use on the oily surface of the canvas and then it is thinned by using finger pressure. If you need to give a plane effect you need to use your fingers as a spatula. If you need to create any stroke you need to use your fingers as a wooden brush. At one time you can create four strokes by using all your fingers. If you want to decrease the darkness of colour you need to move your finger gently by using pressure techniques of the fingers.

Finger oil painting is a new and creative technique in the field of oil painting. The most important thing about it is to keep the surface of the canvas or paper as smooth as the surface of tiles on floor.

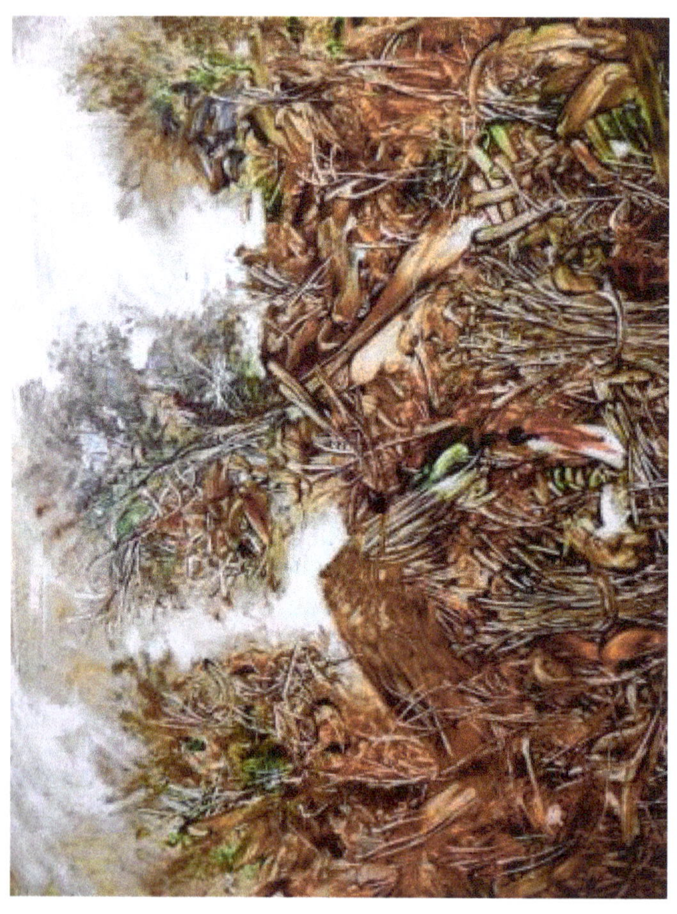

# Time taken in finger oil painting

The most amazing thing in this finger painting is the time taken to complete a painting. In the future, I expect lot from this technique as it takes very less time to finish the painting. In this book, the paintings illustrated have taken approximately fifteen to twenty minutes time to complete one painting.

Same subject of the paintings are similar in their illustration but the subject does not matter. When you start creating strokes with finger the painting can be completed in twenty minutes or less then it.

The surface of the canvas or paper being slippery in touch the colour flows fluently on the paper or canvas. Use all the fingers for creating strokes. Some time you can use both the hands for complicated strokes when all you finger gives a stroke at the same time you are able to get at least four strokes at one time. The time taken can be within one second or more. If you keep on making strokes you can get hundreds of strokes in a minute keeping in mind the more of strokes should be same everywhere but according to the subject.

For exampleto create a cloudy sky use you palm for swift and plane sky or use it according to the clouds in the sky through your imagination.

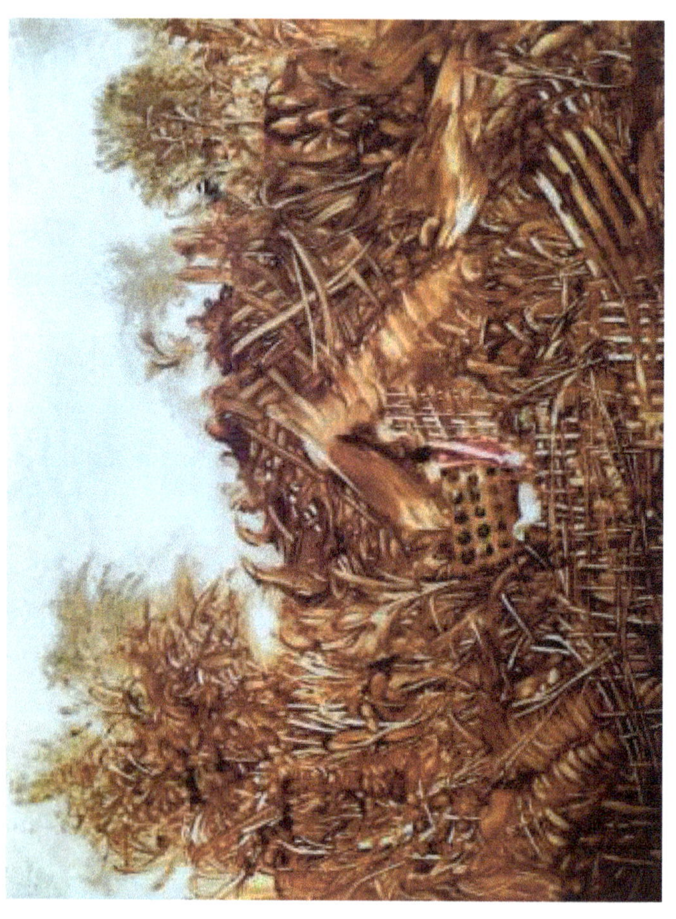

# Technical description of plate-1

Title of the painting- My home

In this painting a hut is depicted with different stokes and a woman in red and white dress is standing and watching her house. First of all use brown (brunt sina) with lot of oil and make the canvas or paper flow with colour. The sky should be decided first.Put your palm hard on the paper and erase it fast as youcan. A tone of light brown colour is created on the paper for creating the hut.Use all your fingers and squeeze it.For highlight use you nail and at last the figure should be painted. Decide the length of the figure and erase it with a piece of cloth.Make it white and take crimson red on the tip of your first finger and rub it hard for creating the dress. White colour should not be used anywhere. White is the surface of the paper or canvas. Use your first fingertips and press it hard wherever you want to give the effect of the dress. At last, white or black which is on the side of the painting is created using rags of cloth. The hair of the women in the figure is painted at last using you first finger tip with a black colour.

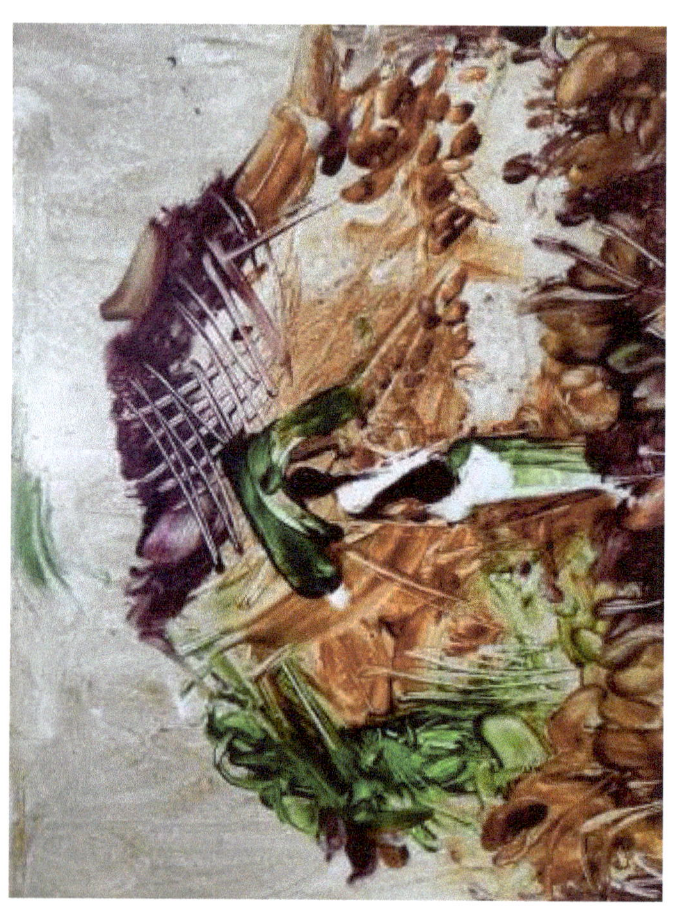

# Technical description of plate-2

Title of the painting- The grass cutter

First of all you put brown colour with lot of linseed oil with the help of your palm or you can use a piece of cloth for it. Just spray brown colour all over the paper or on the canvas with the help of the finger to create strokes to make hut and the base ground. With a piece of cottonfirst erase slightly the part of the sky. Erase gently with cotton so that you get a desired sky colour. Create the figure part withyour nail and erase it hard with the help of the cotton. The outline should be maintained. Take green colour and create the grass bunch with your firstfinger tip.Stroke it hard somewhere to get the light part. Use the black colour with your first finger tip to create the hair of the women carrying the grass. Then you can use green colour to create bushes. For final touch use your nail and make the entire cross or zigzag lines to give it final outlook for more sensation you can use brown colour wherever you want with the help of your first finger tap anywhere. The pressure of the finger should be according the required light and shade of the painting.

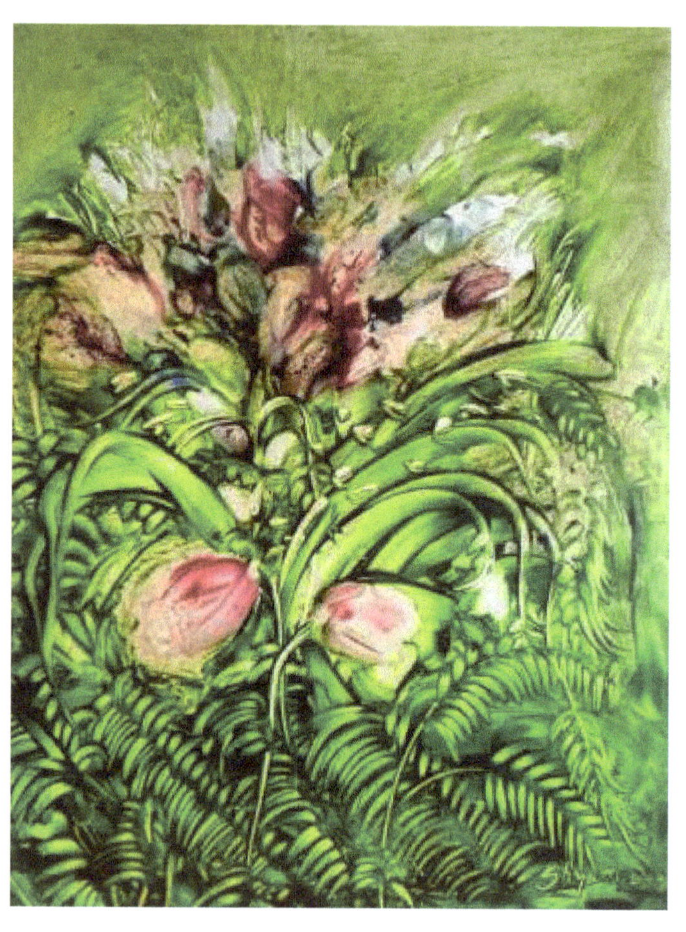

# Technical description of plate-3

## The flower and leaf

For this type of painting use green colour first with sufficient oil all over the paper or canvas and stroke it somewhere with your thumb and fingers to get the effect of green leaf. Set up the arrangement of flowers in your mind and erase it hard with your first finger or you can use a piece of cloth or cotton. The red colour should be applied without using oil. Put red colour wherever you want and with a dry piece of cloth or cotton erase for the white effect. Again I remind that white colour is not used in the finger oil colour painting. For white you have to erase it or buff it. To get the desired effect,use your first finger to make long leaf and the centre of leaf is made by nails. For final touch, first stroke it hard by your all four finger in a very balanced way. The strokes once made can be corrected or changed so white stroke is in your inner sense of painting or yourconscious mind. It should be lightly concentrated on the type of painting you are creating. The time taken in this painting by me was only ten minutes.

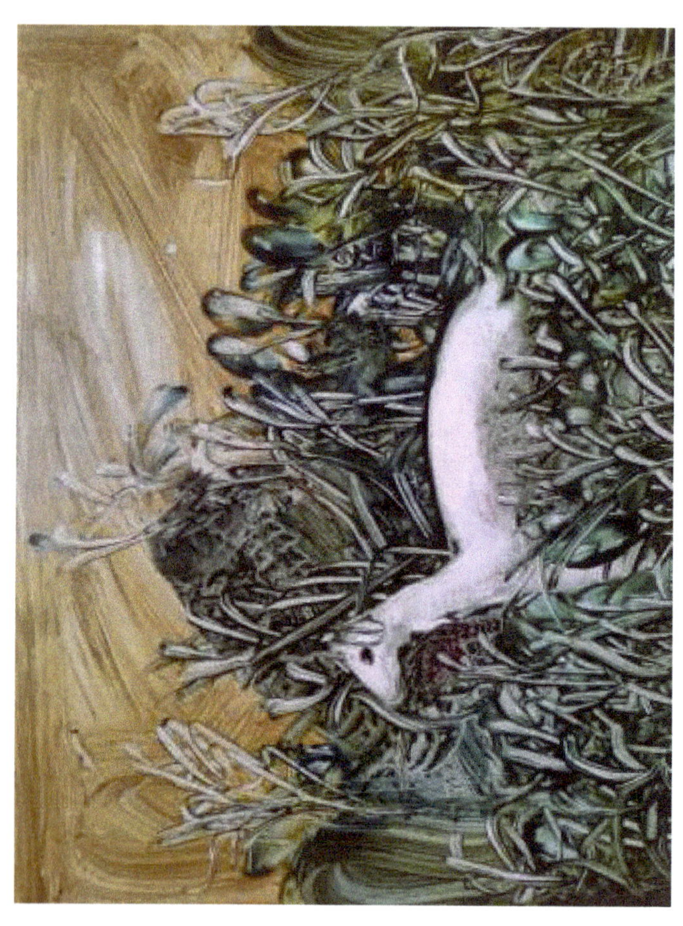

# Technical description of plate-4

In this type of painting, two colours are used simultaneously to create the desired effect. First of all use yellow colour all over the paper or the canvas.Keep in mind the smoother will be the paper or canvas the better will be the stroke. If you see that the paper or canvas is not so smooth you can give one coat of enamel white colour one each paper or canvas. After using the yellow colour, use green colour on it without erasing the green paint. If you use green colour on yellow the result will be green. Start stroking with all your fingers light or hard also use nails for bright effect. The grass should be light somewhere and somewhere very dark so that you can get a better shaded grass. When you finish striking the green part decide the size of the goat on the paper or canvas. The hidden part need not to be done anything. The depicted white part of the goat is erased by the piece of cotton and the eye is spotted with black colour by your first finger for more effect the nails are used for the highest light. When you finish the painting keep it straight on the board. If you slant it or lay it the oil on the paper will start flowing downward which will spoilyour strokes. It needs to be dried in sunlight for two or three days or you can dry it with the help of electric dryer. The drying system is slow in this painting. If you want a fast drying you need to use good quality of oil colour (Wintson Newton oil colour).

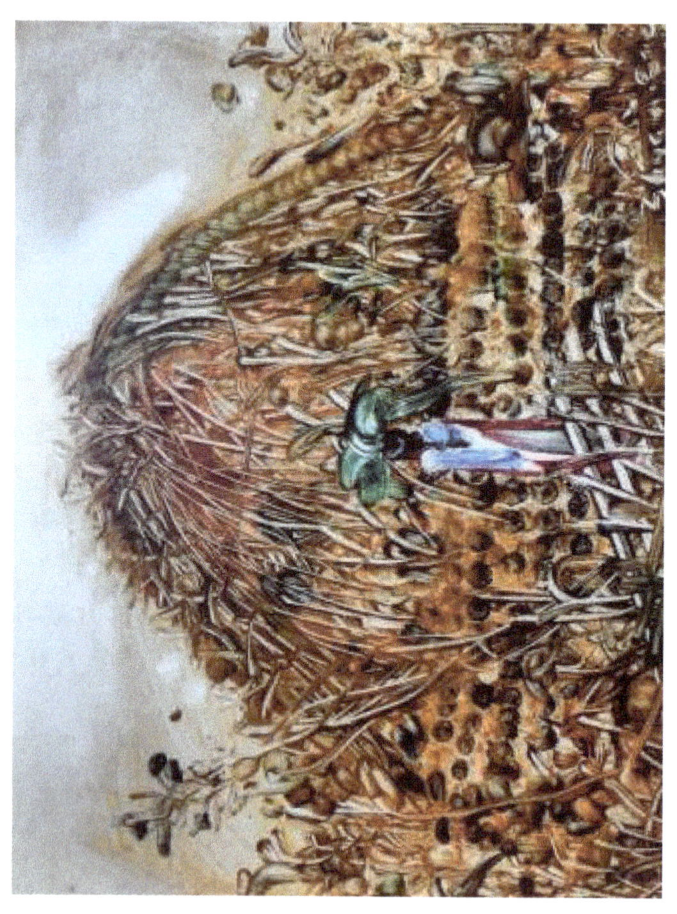

# Technical description of plate-5

## Village grass cutter

In this type of painting you need to use yellow **c**olourfirst with the help of a piece of cloth.For swift and smooth effect use your palm. Decide the size of hut and use brown colour on the area of hut. Use some sap green on desired area. The cow dung on the wall of the hutis spotted by using sap green on the brown colour itself. The fencing of the hut is done through nails. When you complete the painting from sky to hut then decide the size of the grass cutter. Erase it for the decided size of the grass cutter. Red skirt and blue shirt of the women should be painted first. For shades on skirt use pressure technique accordingly. For light use more pressure of finger and for dark use more colour and less pressure. The open hair of the women should be painted at last when the clothes are completed. At last use sap green with your first finger. For the bunch of grass on the head .For more sensation in the work use your nails for the bamboos used in hut. Squeeze with your entire finger for the effect of dry bushes whoever you want. At last if you want a distinct sky wipe more hard with the cotton for the highlighted sky. Dry it on a straight board for at least two to three days in sunlight or use electric dryer for one to two hours.

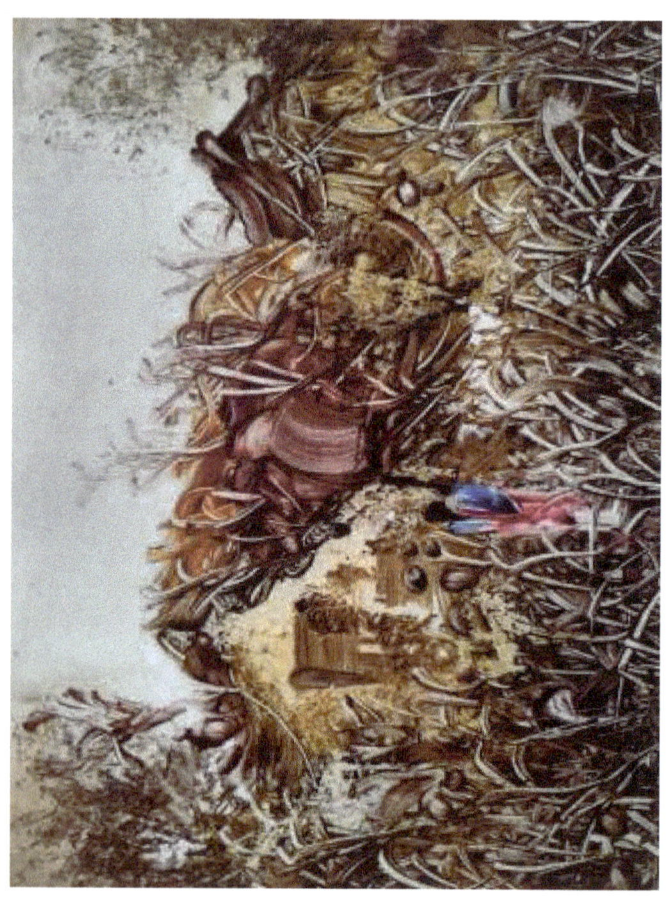

# Technical description of plate-6

## The old home

In this type of painting, use the darkest colour like dark brown first with appropriate oil on the paper or canvas. Spread the dark brown colour with the help of the fingerflat on the surface. Decide the area of hut and sky. Wipewith a piece of cloth the required sky area and start the strokes from the roof of the hut with all your fingers. The front wall of the hut is very light in colour and it seems very old. For the front wall, take a little bit of turpentineoil and drop it gently on the wall surface area. Spread gently, andif it starts excessive spreading, wipe the colour by your fingers leaving the area for the door part. For better result tilt the paper or canvas gently downwards. A net or a crank type effect will be created due to the dropping of turpentine oil downwards. Afterward, take some brown or dark brown and give some strokes by your three fingers side by side to control the excess oil spread. At last, decide the size of the figure and wipe it with a piece of cloth. The wiped area will be dried so use the colour without using oil. The Prussian blue and crimson red in the cloth is used by the first finger. The hair of the lady is painted at last with a stroke of black colour. For more sensational effect wipe with a rag of cloth the sky area and buff the side of the hut with dark brown colour. At last, highlight the painting with your nails. Scratch it wherever you want to create the desired effect.

# Technical description of plate-7

**Goats in rain**

For this type of paintings, it needs some extra control on texture of colour. The brown colour is spread carelessly on the surface of smooth canvas or paper. Sap green colour is also used somewhere for long grass. Put the Sap green colour here and there and make the stems of the long grass with your nails. When you get a wet type effect, spray turpentine oil or thinner with the help of your finger and watch the effect for some time. Keep on putting the strokes here and there. Theremaining spotswill be decided for the placing of goat. You can sketch the goat with your nails if you want. Wipe the area of goat where youwould like to give white and gray tones.Witha very balanced stroke of your finger tips, paint the eye of the goat.

The dropping effect should be done carefully. Turpentine oil is not too thick or heavy.You can spray turpentine oil with the help of spray gun. For drying the painting, be careful that the colour does not spread out of canvas or paper. The toning of white colour in goats can be done by the appropriate pressure of finger. Press the finger hard and wipe gently where you would like to get highlights. The pressure of the finger will be the most important part of finger painting with oil colour. Dry the painting using dryer or sunlight.

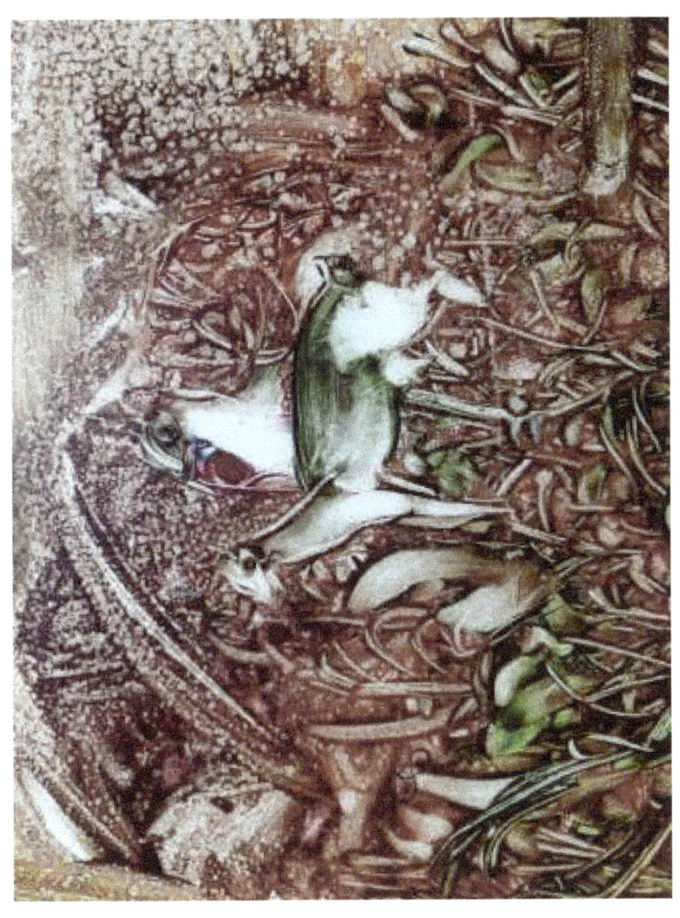

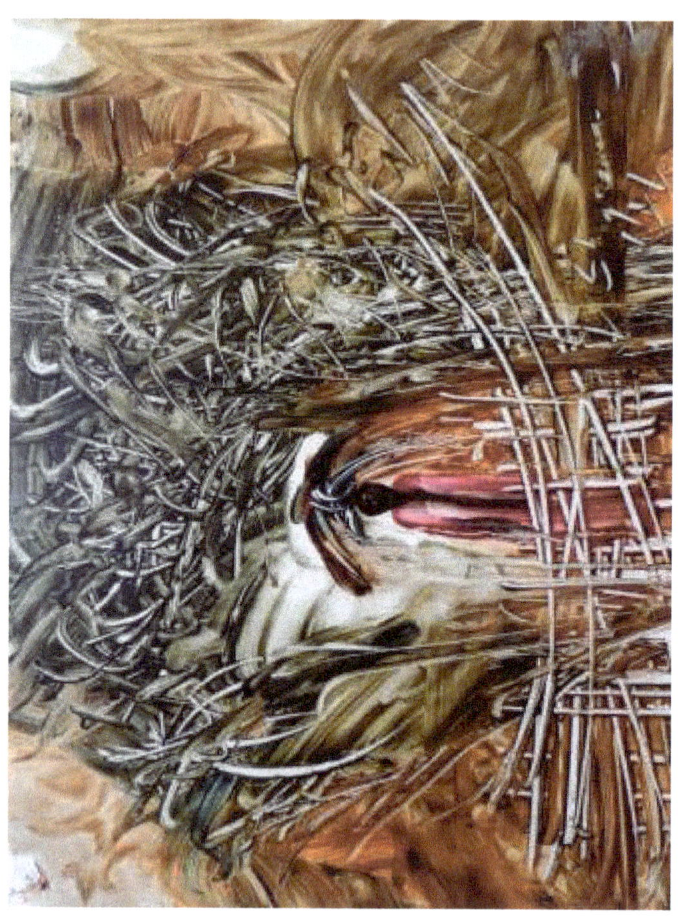

# Technical description of plate-8

## Grass cutter inside the fence

For this type of painting, use Bursting brown and Sap green. First of all, use brown colour with your finger carelessly and keep on creating strokes then with the Sap green afterwards. Sap green will be used for creating the effect of the tree. When you create the background, wipe the centre area for the figure. Wipe it hard so that the area is dried.Without using oil in the colour, put the red colour with your finger tip and give an effect of clothes. When you get an effect of clothes create the head of the women with black colour. Then you can put the bundle of grass on her head using brown and then Sap green. At last, you work on the fence. The fencing stroke is done by the nails. Put all your fingers at the same time on the canvas or paper and scratch hard by four or more strokes. Give some horizontal strokes and some vertical strokes to create a net type or a graphtype effect. If you observe closely, you can see the lines of the fence, horizontal line or vertical line and some vertical line on horizontal line. At last you can put some strokes with your nails. You can watch this painting on You-Tube (Shyam Das finger Painting).

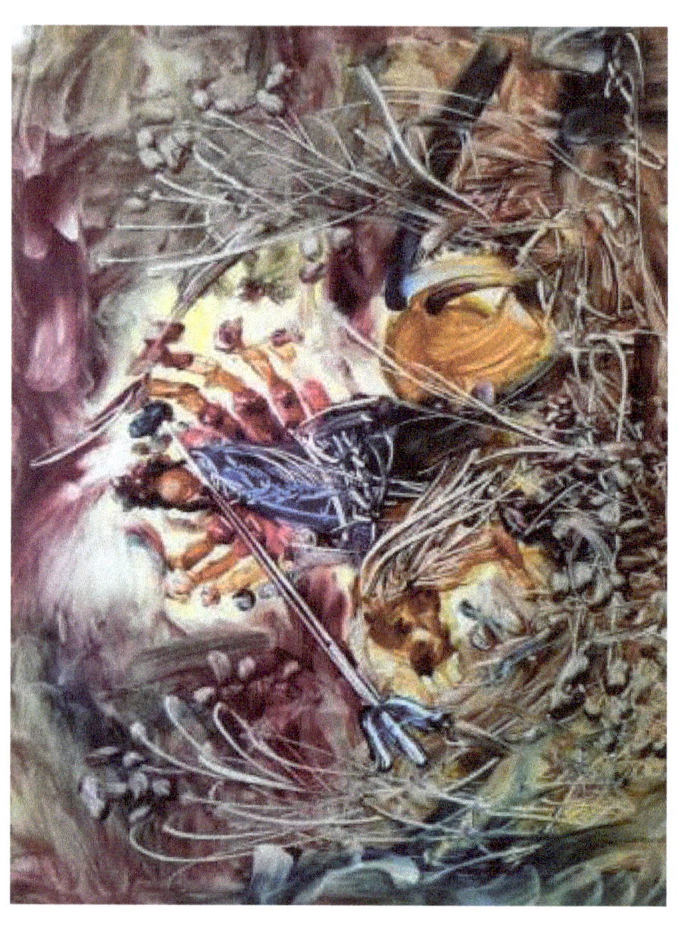

# Technique description of plate-9

**Durga**

For this type of painting, the use of oil is very less. Don't use much oil. The surface of the paper or canvas should be very swift. For this type use colour only with one or two fingers. For the base you can use yellow colour which should be applied very thinly with the help of the turpentine oil. First of all create all the strokes with finger or nail and then you create the figure of durga. The colour texture should be thick while using the colour. First use the red colour and then the blue on it. The lion should be painted after you create the image of durga. Where you see you are not getting the proper effect you can wipe the colour with the tip of the cloth. If you paint in abstract it needs no correction but if you paint in realistic you need to be very careful and the wiping method works more in realistic painting. The trishul or the spear in the hand of Durga should be done lastly with your nails. After using the nails for line work the painting should be completed. This painting is imaginary, So the perfection in image and the lion is not maintained. Only the form is maintained in the painting. The bright light on the background indicates supernatural power.

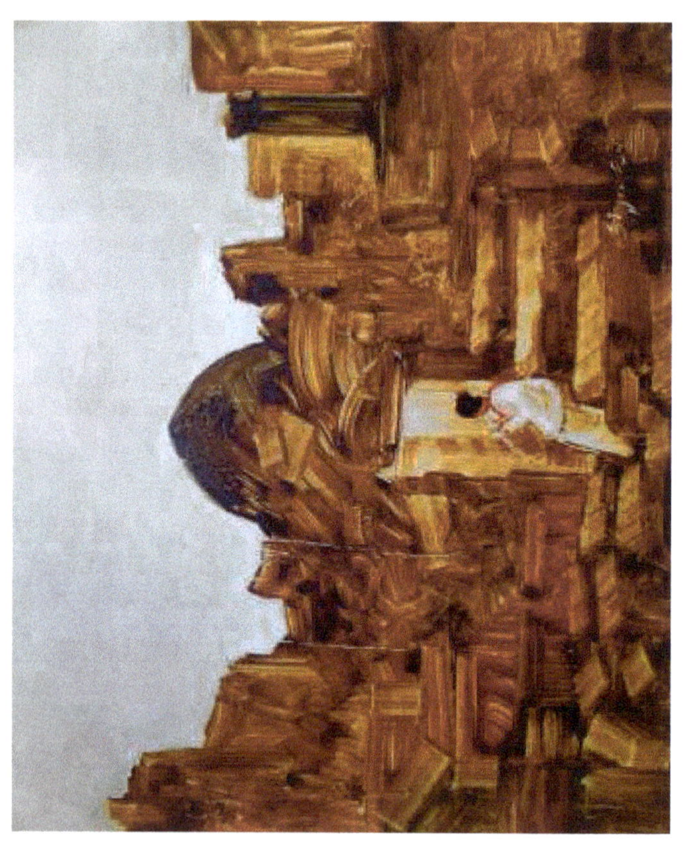

# Technical description of plate-10

## The Flute player

In this type of paintings,first of all, create the monument using some rugs of cloth filled with brown color and use turpentine oil for the base. The sky is also in the same colour used as in the monument. The sky is very light due to the thinness in the colour. Most of the work in the monument is done by the rugs of clothes. Use finger tips or nail for prominent line work. For the sky, use yourpalm. The palm should be used with high pressure so that the effect of colour is highlighted. At last decide the size of the flute player sitting on the stairs. Wipe the area of the player with a thin piece of cloth. To paint the head of the women use dark black colour with your first finger tip. The line on the flute is done by the nail. Putting your signature on the painting should be done when the painting is not dried hard. Put your signature by your nail when the painting is semi dried. The effect of finger painting not only depends on the oil but also on the pressure of the fingers.

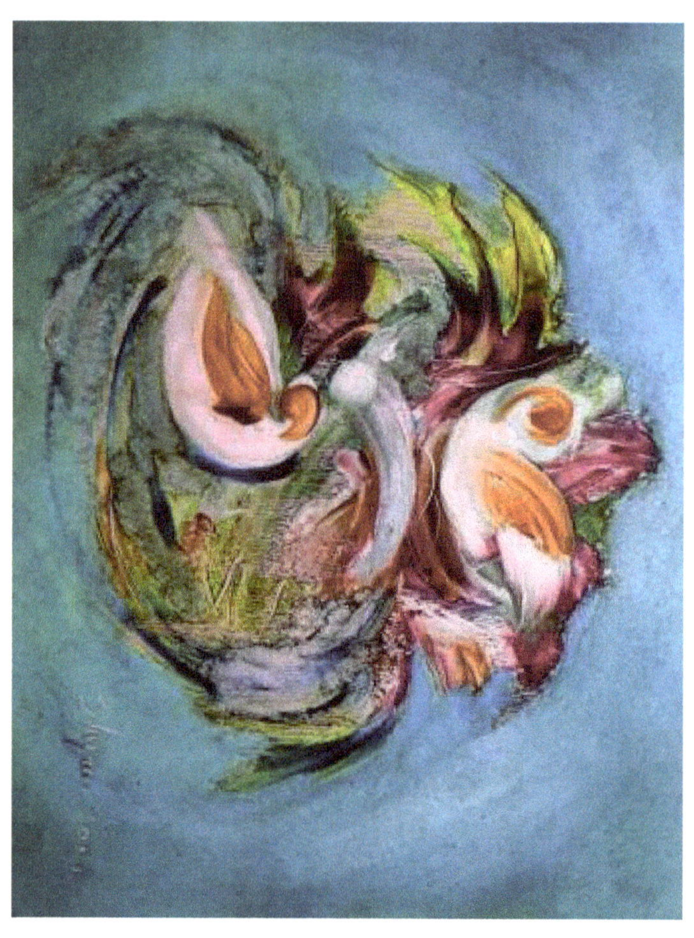

# Technical description of plate-11

**Pigeonpair**

In this type of paintings, you mainly need to use your palm. Put Linseed oil on the paper and a Cobalt blue colour and start rubbing it vigorously withyour palm. When the colour is evenly spread then create the nest of the pigeonwith your finger tips. Take some red colour and a very little yellow and some green onyourfirst, second and third finger tip and start strokes simultaneously. When you get the created nest image, use the wipe method for the pigeon. Wipe the image of pigeon. If you want you can create an outline of the pigeonwith your nails. When the outline of the pigeon is completed, wipe the colourfrom the canvas or paper. Make it white on the surface of the paper or the canvas. For sensational image, take Brown colour on your finger tip and rub it for the feather of the pigeon and the head in an abstract form. The oil on the canvas or paper should be used very less so that the flowing of oil is prohibited. In this type, the flow of oil and tremendous strokes of finger are not needed. The palm and the oil have the most important use. The palm of the hand should be used evenly and the oil in a very limited proportion so that the colour gets merged in the oil itself. There are endless types in finger oil painting and the strokes developed are so unique that it can't be done by any brush. The time taken for this painting was 15 minutes.

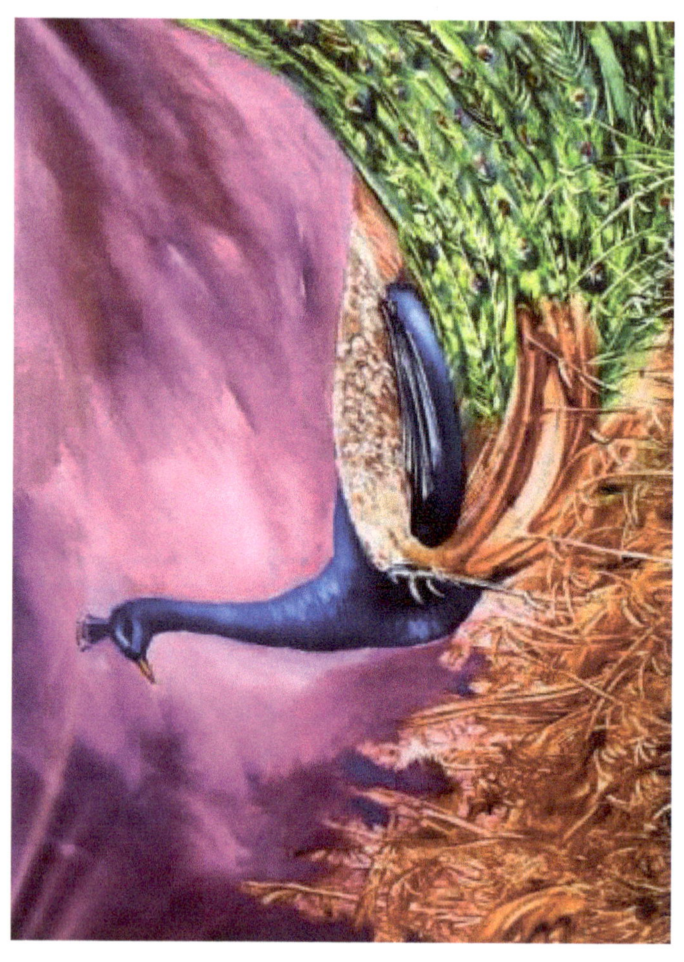

# Some important feature of the oil finger painting

1. In oil finger painting, the surface of the canvas or the paper should be so smooth that the
2. colour slips on the canvas.
3. The coating method of oil colour is not applicable on this type.
4. Light colour is used first on the canvas as it is the opposite of oil painting.The dark shades are then used by thickening of the colour and using less oil.
5. The thinning of the colour is done by using more oil till the required effect is produced.
6. All the fingers are used in this type. The nails are also an important tool for this type. The pressure of the finger tips and the pressure of the nails are used in a very balanced way.
7. The most important characteristic of this type is that there is no use of white colour at all. To get the effect of white colour only wiping method is used. This is done by wiping the surface with appropriate pressure needed.
8. Drying of finger oil painting is done by keeping the painting straight on the surface board. Tilting of canvas or paper can spoil the strokes as the oil may flow.

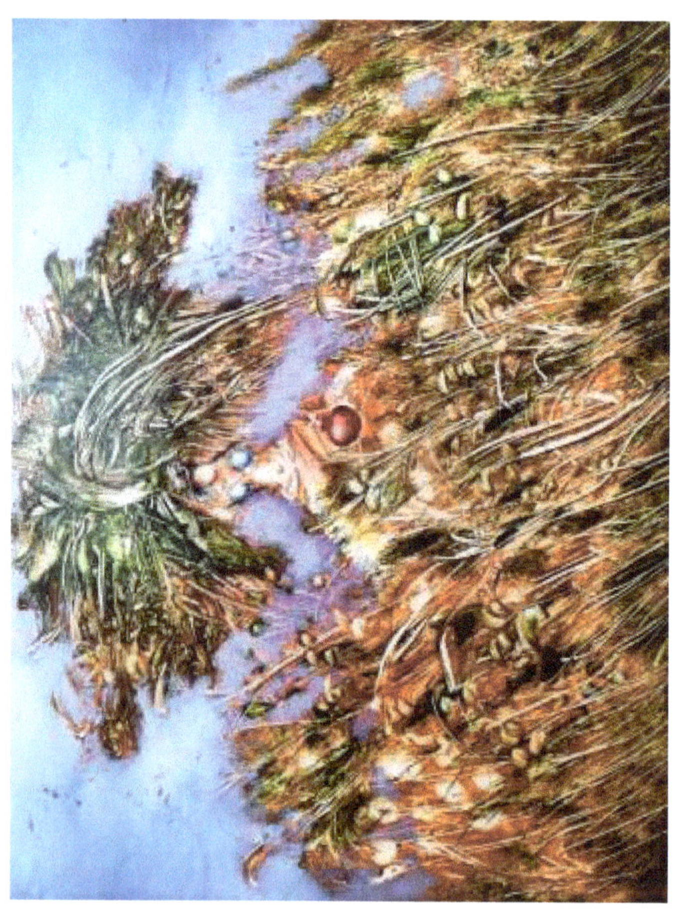

# The base of the finger oil paintings and the difference from all the other paintings

This process of painting is different from the all other types of paintings because the method and techniques used are completely different. The process is so fast that creating anything can be so easy thata person who is not an artist can also create something by using this method. It needs no pre-planned things. It gives creation at the same time you start painting. Put the oil on canvas and mix the colour carelessly on it with surplus oil, you can get an image at that time. The image you get during thattime,you get a new painting. Forexample, the oil on canvas is flowing here and there and you quickly put some colour on your finger tip and make move it around with your senses. You will get an image. The image you get will give a start to a new painting. If you use only one finger and move around you will at least get an image of a reptile or a flower plant. The pressing of colour or scratching the colour with your finger will also give a new image. The image you see on canvas will give birth to a new painting. This is a new way of creating for beginners. It needs only your self-consciousness.

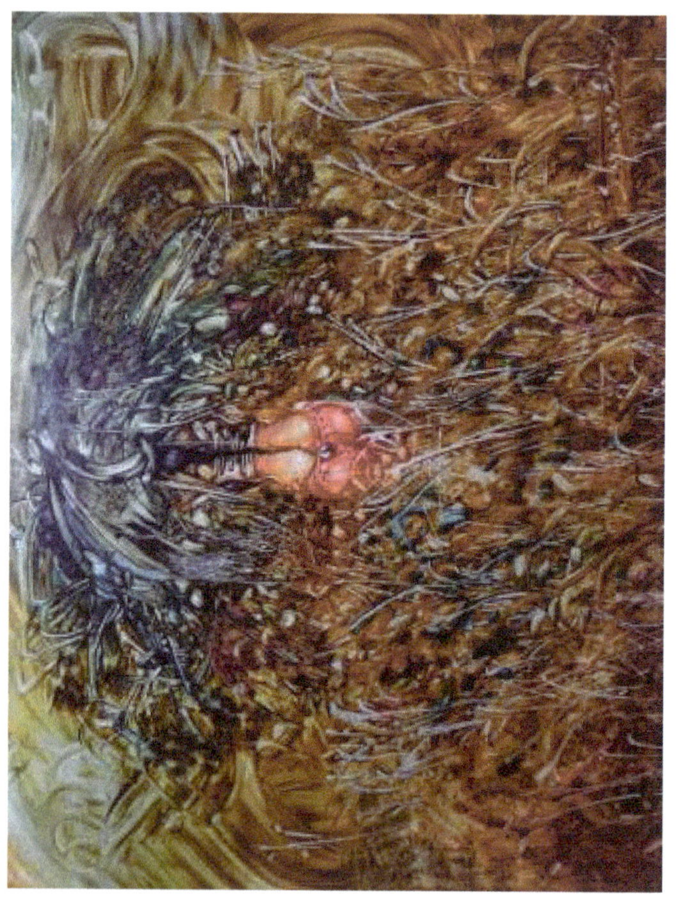

# Abstract paintings by finger oil painting 1

Finger oil painting is one of the best methods for abstract paintings. In abstract paintings, the creation is done in mind before you paint anything but through the technique of finger oil painting you can create anything when you start to work or even you can close your eyes for new creation. Put the oil on the paper and takeout the colour direct from tube and put it anywhere on the canvas. Forcolorful creation put different colours at different places on the canvas or paper. Close your eyes and rub the colour with both of your hand carelessly swinging your hand up and downallover the canvas. Open your eyes and the newly createdimage can be seen. Don't use finger strokes first. Do it by your palm till you set a desired imaginary image. Now use your finger tips for new types of colour texture and images. Put your entire finger and just contract it fast. The new image with many strokes can be produced at the same time. For different types of paintings you can use the side of the palm and move it hard up or down or in any direction you want. The new type of stroke will be created on the canvas. Quickly combine every stroke to give a better outlook. The combination of strokes of palm, the side of the palm and the four fingers including the thumb will itself create something new,use your imagination for any new form. Your imagination power will give a new look in all the new stroke combination. For this type you can see plate 12.

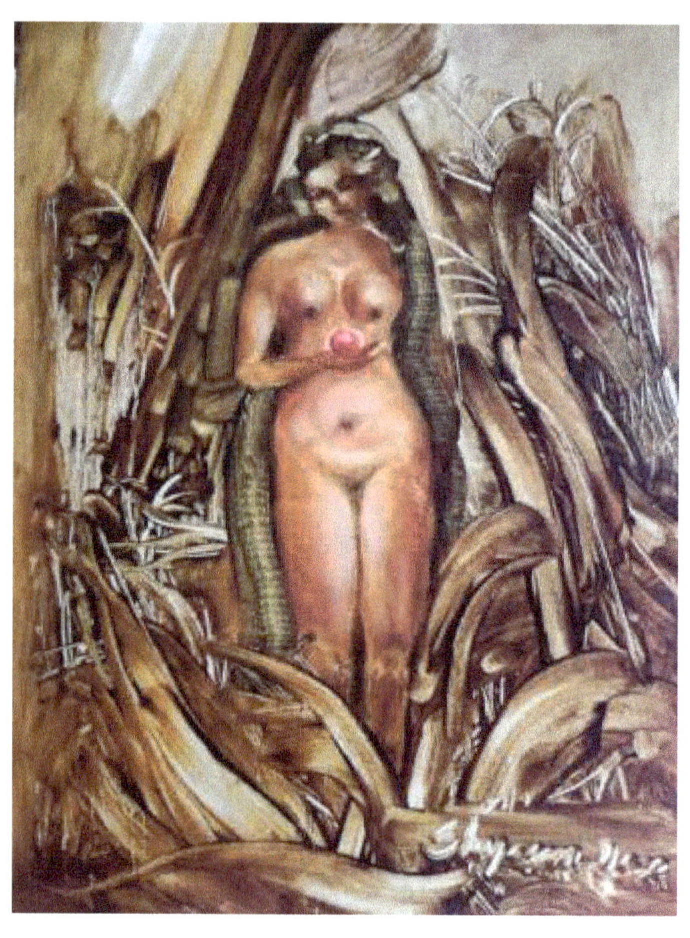

# Technical description for photography finished painting. (Plate-12)

For highly finished and photography finishing the use of fingers and palm need to be balanced. You have to use a piece of foam for doing so. The finger tips used in this technique is using your finger tip as a rubber. For these types of paintings the oil on the canvas should be sprayed with the hip of the foam. Put the colour on the deserved place. First create the figure by using brown colour. The use of oil should be very less.

First of all create the figure and highlight the brown colour using dry piece of foam. When you punch the foam on brown colour the colour itself become highlighted. Then you can use the wipe method to create the figure distinct and clear. In this process only the finger tip of the first finger is in use.

At last use black colour to control the light part. Just rub the finger tips with dark brown colour without using any oil. There is no need to use all the fingers together to create strokes. Only the first finger tip is used in this technique. For better understanding please see plate 12. (Eve with an apple). Since the oil is used in less amount you can dry this painting keeping the canvas straight on the shelf.

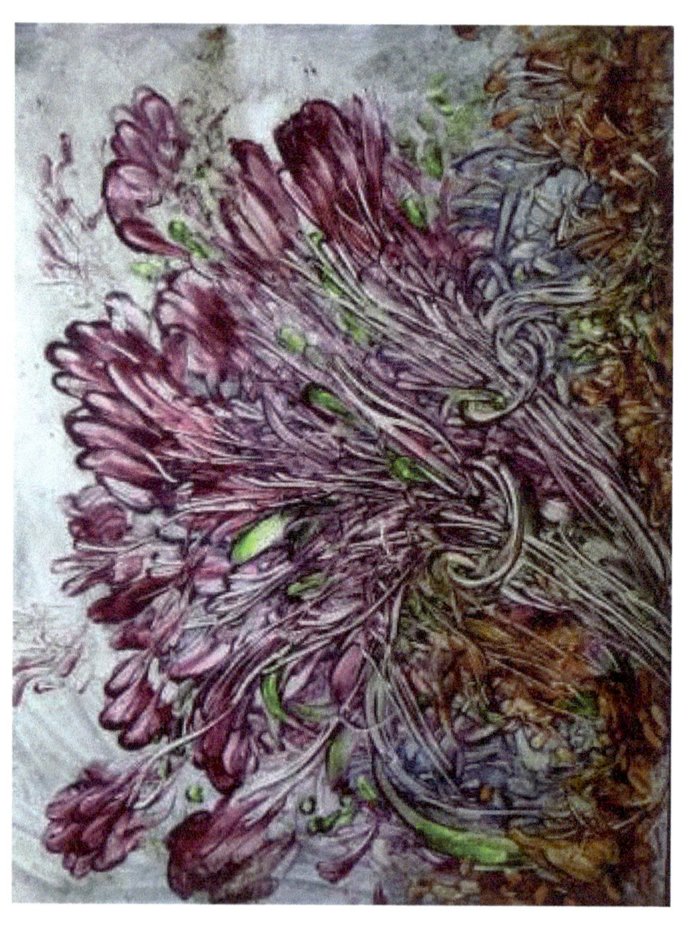

# Process of colour creation in finger painting

Colour creating process in finger painting is a very interesting method. It is not necessary to make the proper colour for the required type of painting. The basic colour that is red, yellow, blue and black are the most used colour in this type of painting. White colour is not used in this oil painting.

White colour which is not used in this painting does not mean that we will not see white in this painting. There is a technique which is used to give white effect and that is simply by erasing that area in the painting. It is erased by a piece of cloth by using turpentine oil. For example If you want to use light yellow then you don't have to mix white with yellow but simply by using yellow colour first and then buff it with a piece of foam or cloth to make it lighter. The buffing of colour is a very important part to create light or dark shades. Suppose you want a greenish effect then use the blue colour on the yellow colour partly as the painting progresses using linseed oil. The mixing of yellow with blue will give you the greenish colour. If you want a very light greenish effect then buff it with a piece of foam. If you want a dark effect then rub it with your finger tip as required.

## Sketching method in Finger painting

Sketching is not necessarily important in finger oil painting. If you want to sketch something or make a layout, you need to use only the colours and not any pencil. Suppose you want to create a village scene then you need to create a hut, pond, cows and buffaloes. In this type of painting you can use yellow colour for making a layout. Put linseed oil on paper or canvas more than surplus and just buff it with a piece of cloth for even distribution of oil on the surface. Take yellow colour on your finger tip and start sketching the subject. Yellow colour is preferred because any colour (dark colour) will naturally merge on this colour. You need not erase or do any type of correction on the sketch. If you see any mistake in the sketch you should not correct it by erasing. You can use the dark colour on the sketch for further improvement. Make the subject first then the background. Once you finish making subject take a piece of cloth and buff the surrounding for creatingbackground. You can use the same piece cloth for creating background which is dipped in the required colour. Just buff it everywhere on the background portion. If you feel that you need darker background you can use the same colour by rubbing with the tip of the first finger. If you want a light effect of the colour, buff it with the piece of cloth. To draw lines you can use your nails to draw these lines. The outline will be white in colour as the nail will remove the colour and the white part of the enamel coated canvas or paper will come out.

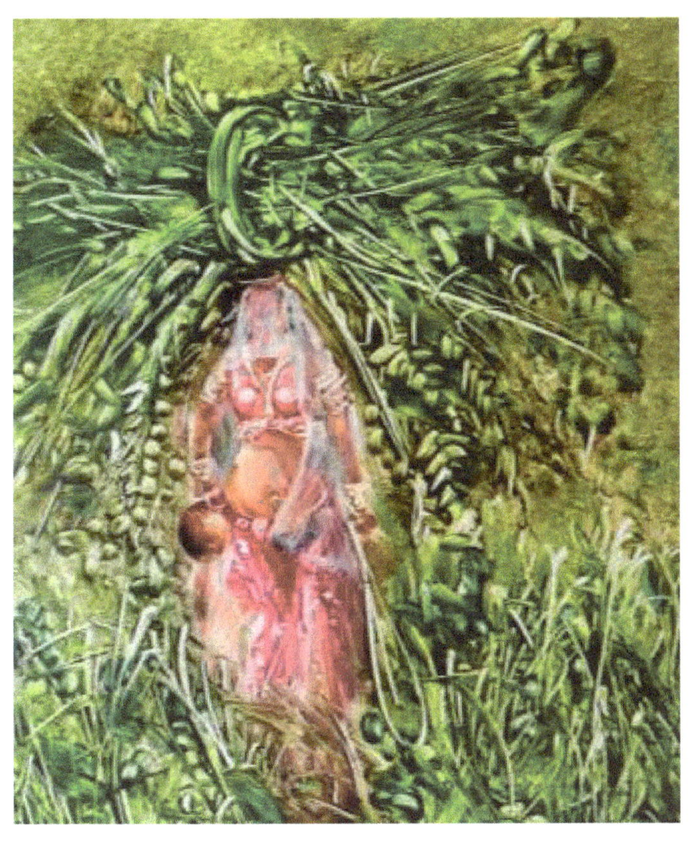

# Abstract painting method in finger oil painting 2

Painting any abstract thing is very easy and the process is very easy. First of all put the linseed oil on the enamel coated canvas or paper and buff it evenly. Put the colour direct on the surface. Put all the three colours red, blue and yellow anywhere you want .Use the middle part of your palm for this type of painting. You can use back of your palm for creative effect. Just start rubbing the colour by both of your palm. Use one palm for one colour and the other for other colour. Rub it hard and fast, you will notice a new type of image. You can create the image by yourself or you can use the created image for a new composition. For a new creation use a new technique. Put some linseed oil on the canvas or paper anywhere you want and mix it slightly with the finger tip and turn the canvas upside down. The colour where you have used the linseed oil later will start flowing or dropping slowly. Now just observe the mode of the dropping colour. You will see a new colour has evolved in this process. Let the colour drop by itself and when you want to turn the mode of dropping then change the position of the canvas.Tilt it a bit and you will see a new colour and a new image is created. If you want to place a realistic image anywhere, just take a piece of cloth and rub that part which is required for that image. The erased part will be white as the canvas is white. Take a little colour on your first finger tip and make any image as you will make on a white surface. The most important part of this technique is to take control over the spread oil on the surface. To take control on the oil surface is not very difficult. If you need thicker colour then reduce the oil by buffing with a piece of cotton and if you need thinner colour then add more oil on the surface.

# Some description on creating grass bunch

In this series of woodcutter or the grasscutter the most important part of the painting is the bunch of grass.To select these subjects is to create a new type of grass bunch. Thestrokes used in creating grass bunch are the most typical part of the finger painting.The strokes produced in the grass bunch can only be done by finger oil painting. It is not possible to create such strokes by any brush or spatula. It is the easiest parts of the technique. Just put the colour on the paper or canvas and add oil and scratch by using your four fingers and using a little bit of thumb.It can be created within a second. If you move your finger slowly you will get a wooden bunch of grass and if you do it fast then you will get a grassy effect. If you move your finger pressing here and there you will get a leafy bunch effect. If you use your nail here and there you will get a stick type grass effect. This is one time stroke effect. If you scratch the same place again and again or continuously you will get a new and creative effect all the time. The second important part in this figure is the woman carrying the grass. There are not any strokes on the woman's cloth. To give a smooth effect on the cloth use your first finger tip and rub the colour gently. For smooth effect it is very important to keep your concentration on the pressure of the finger tips. For the effect of both light and dark shade the same colouris used. There is no mixing of white and black colour. For light effect just buff the colour with a small piece of cotton. Keep practicing this process .Once you become expert you don't need any piece of cloth.

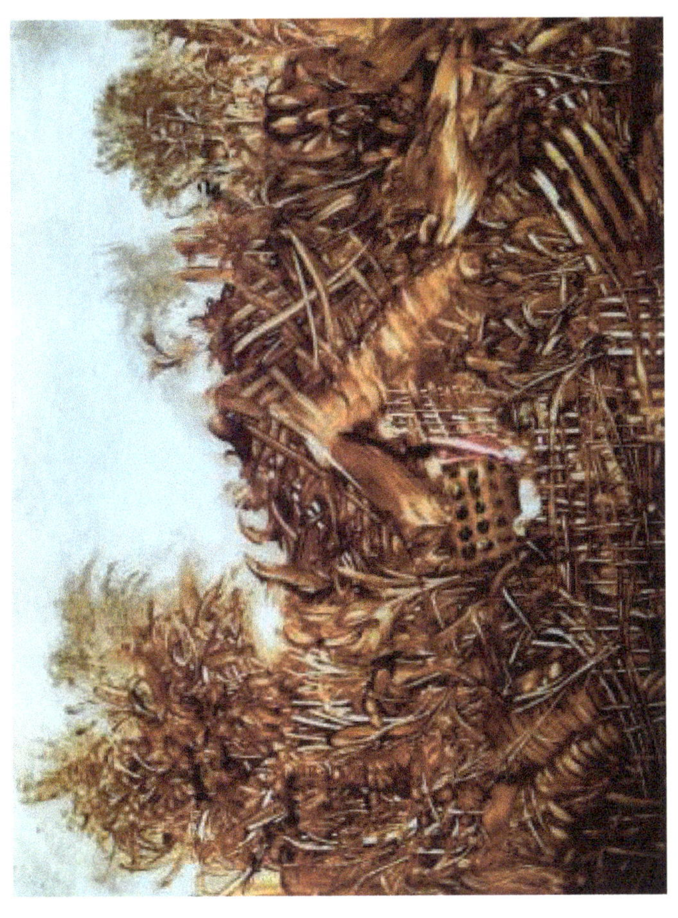

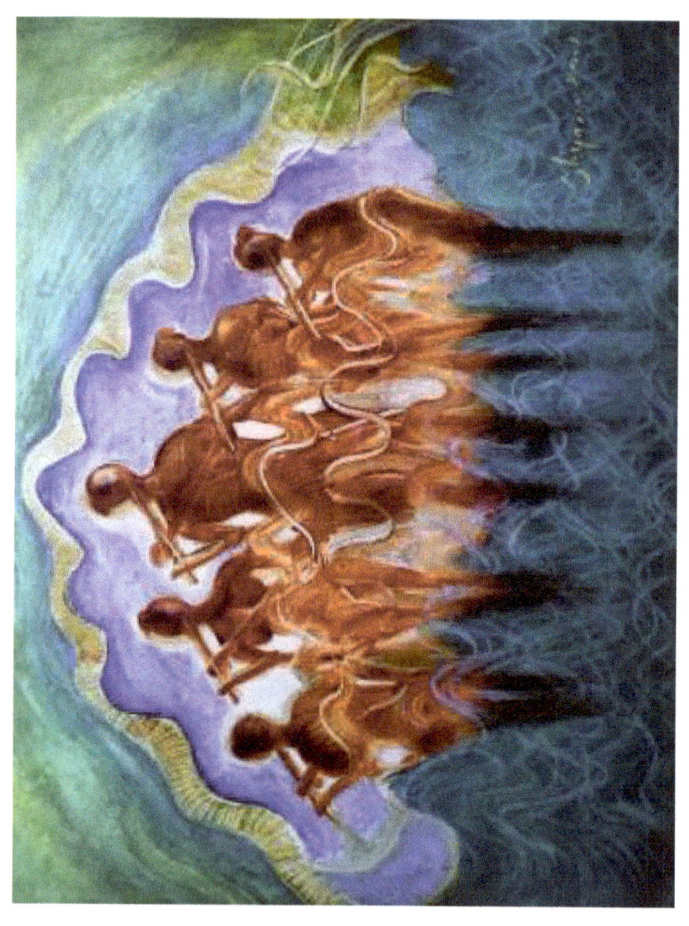

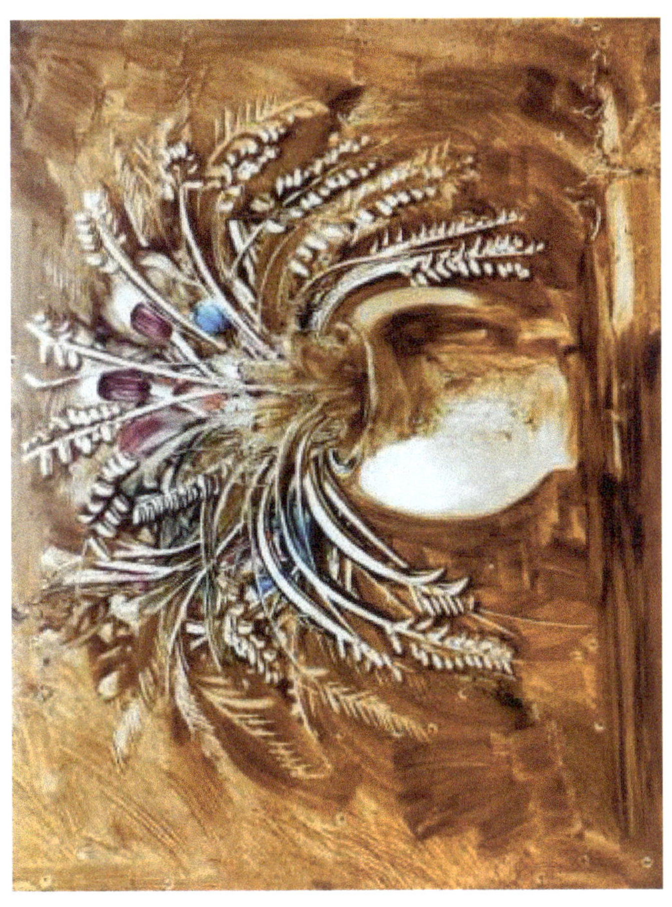

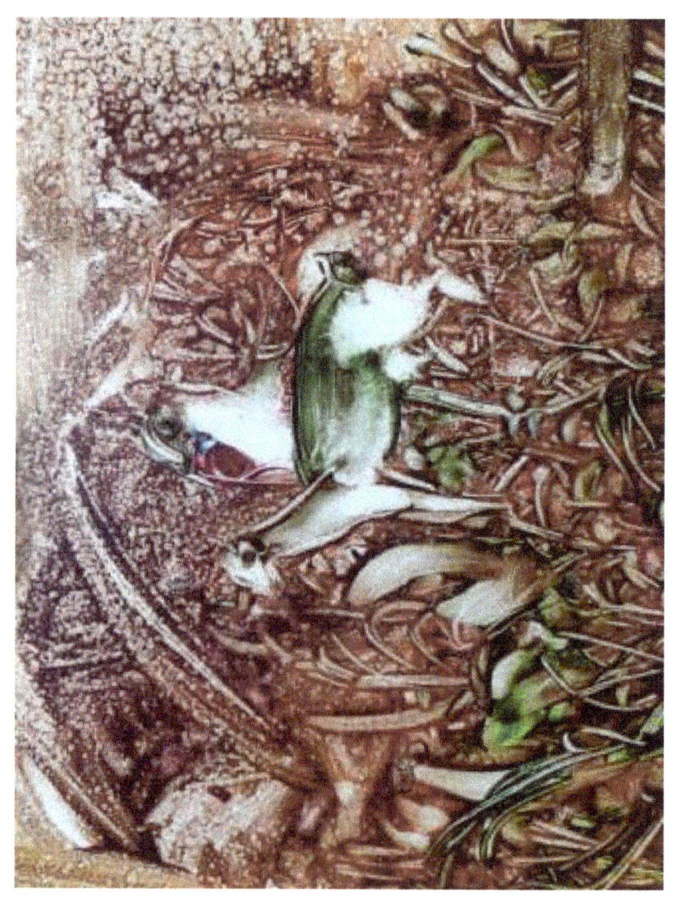

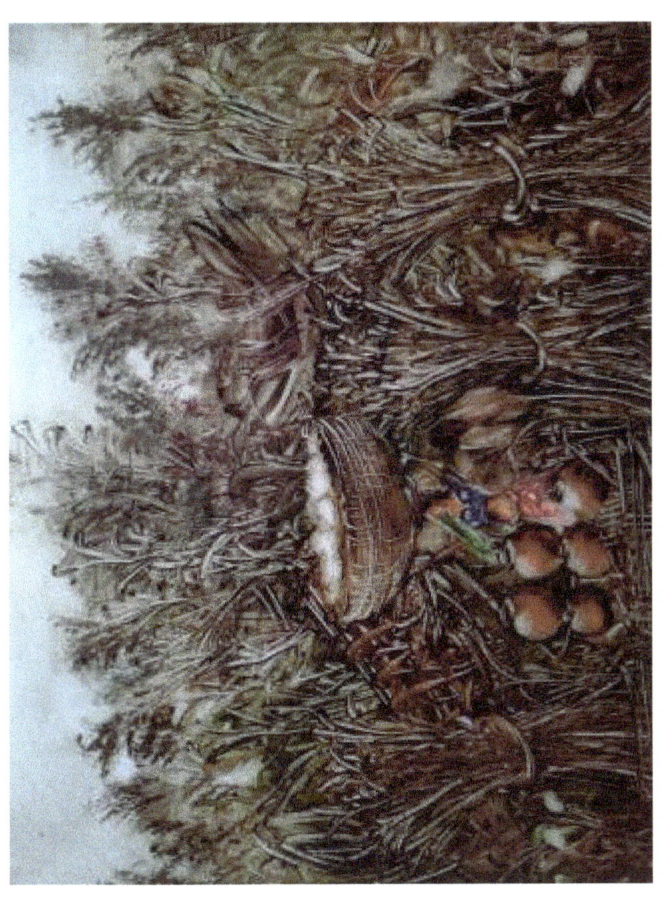

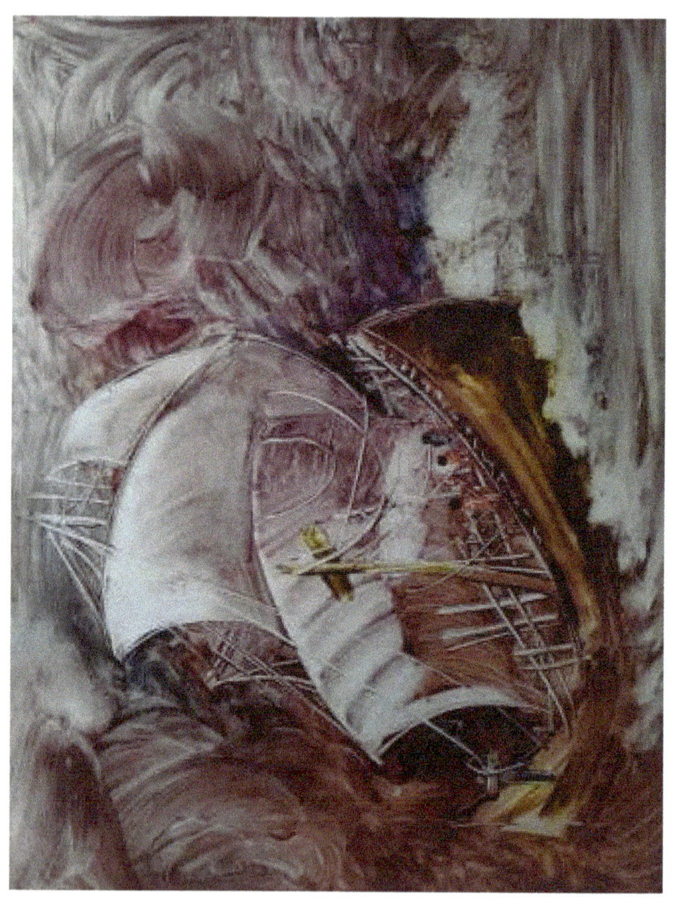

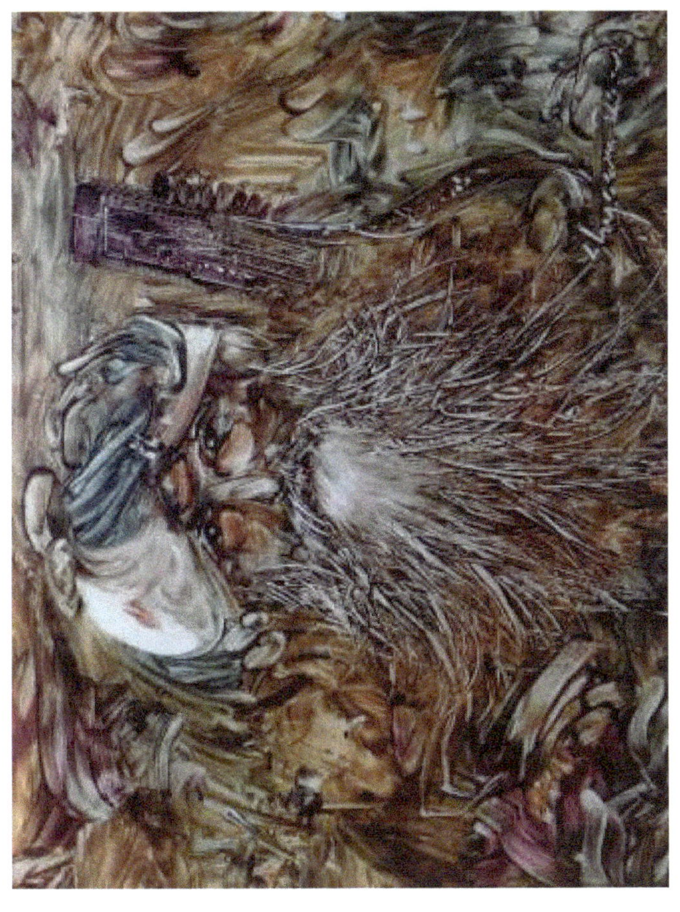

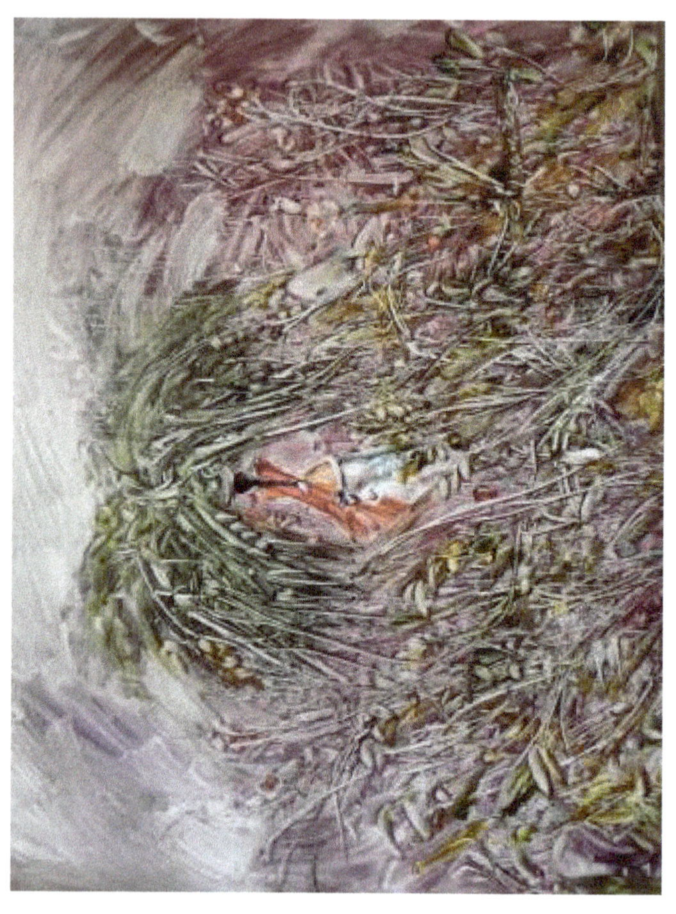

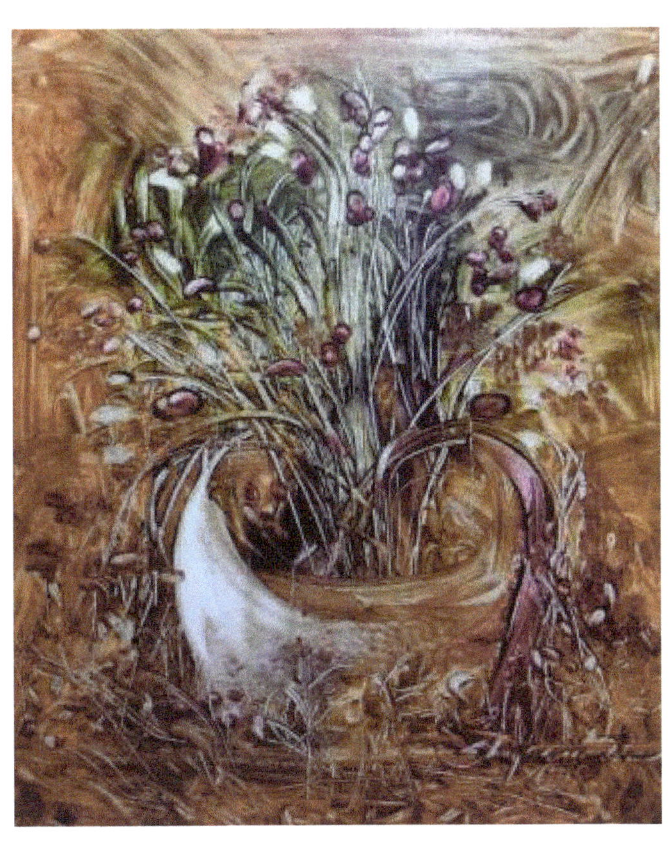

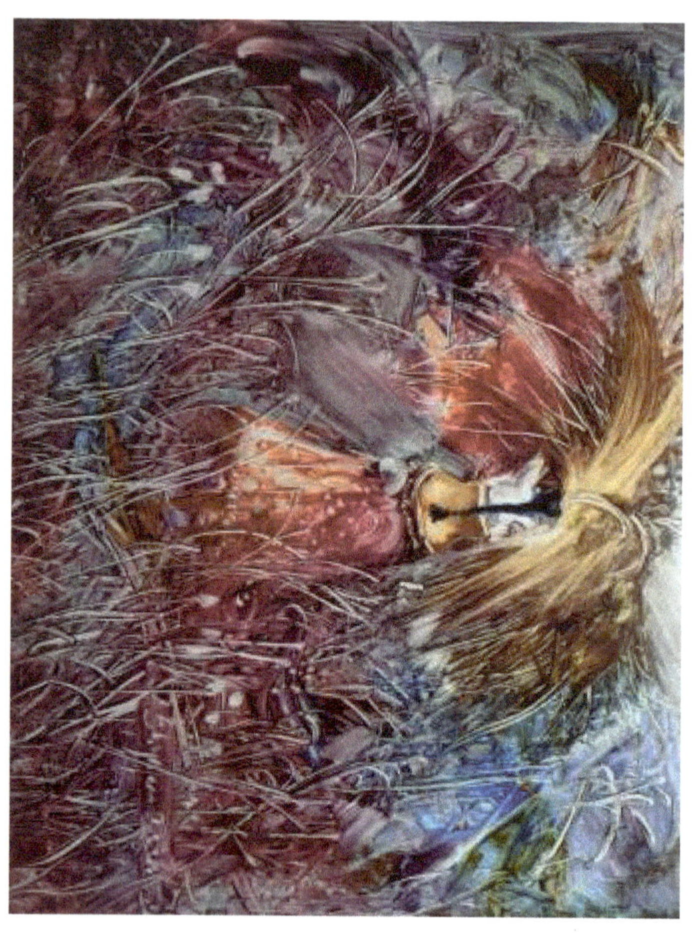

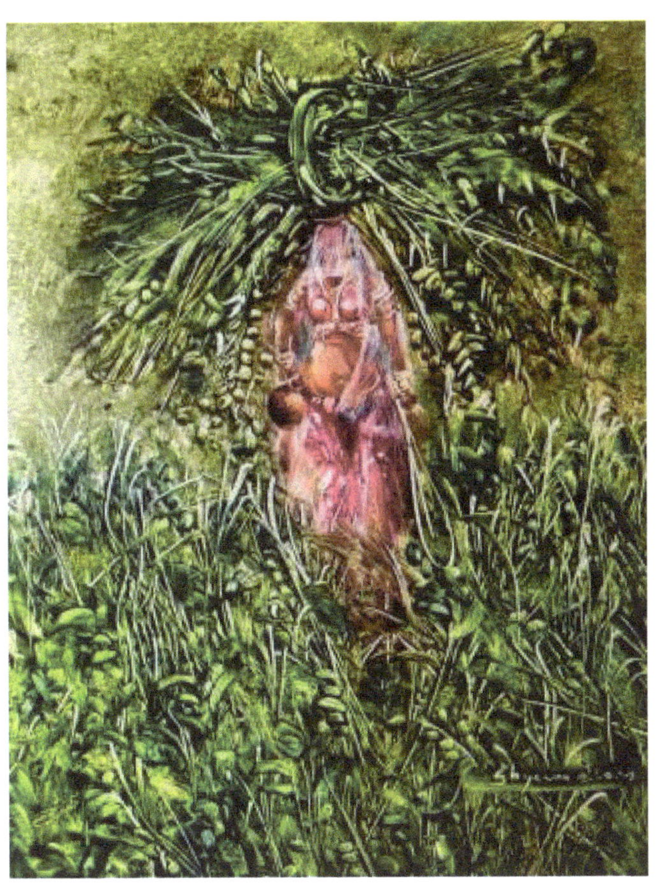

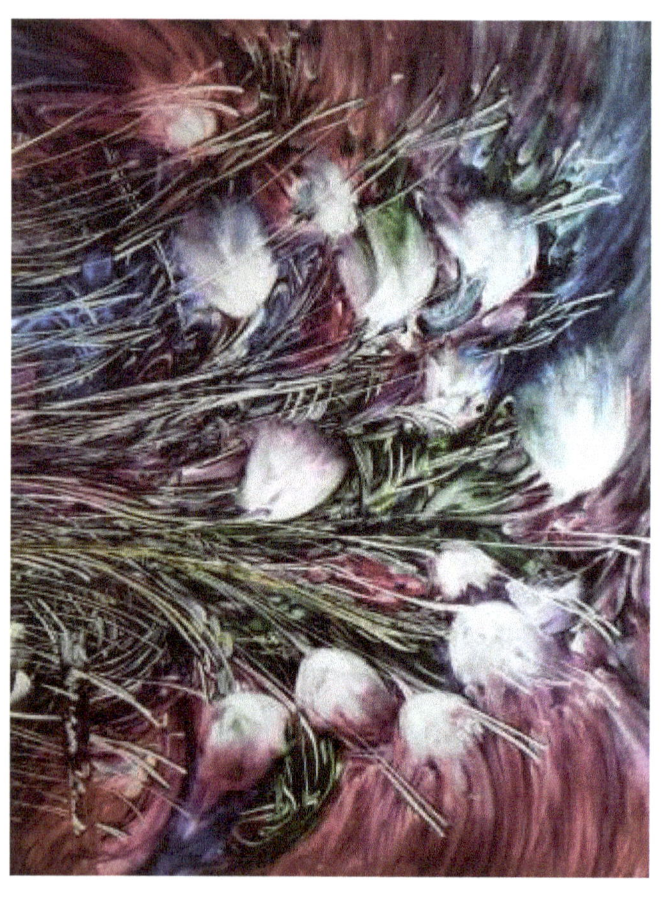

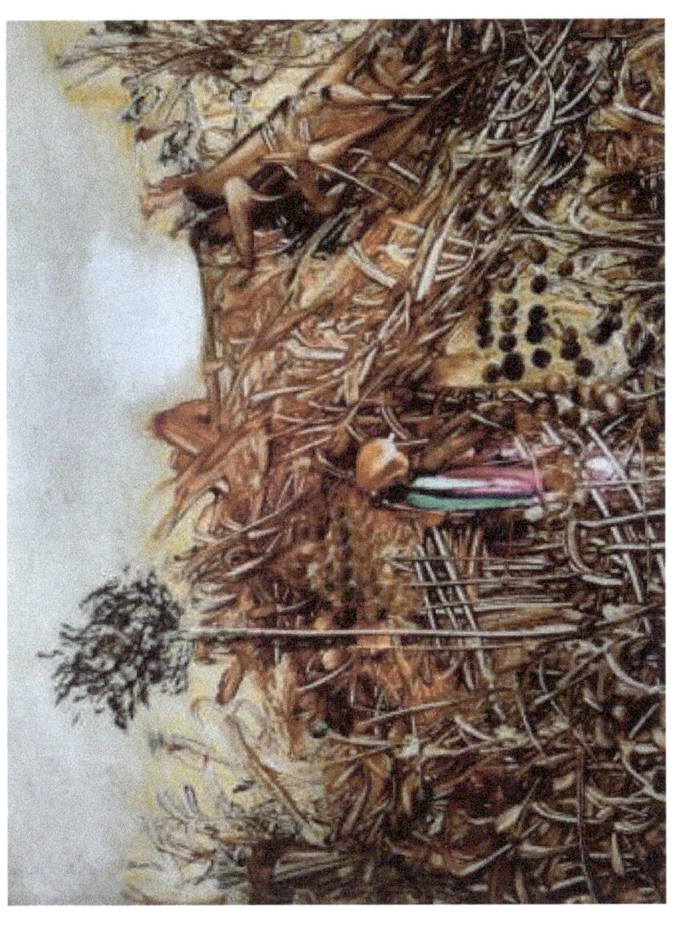

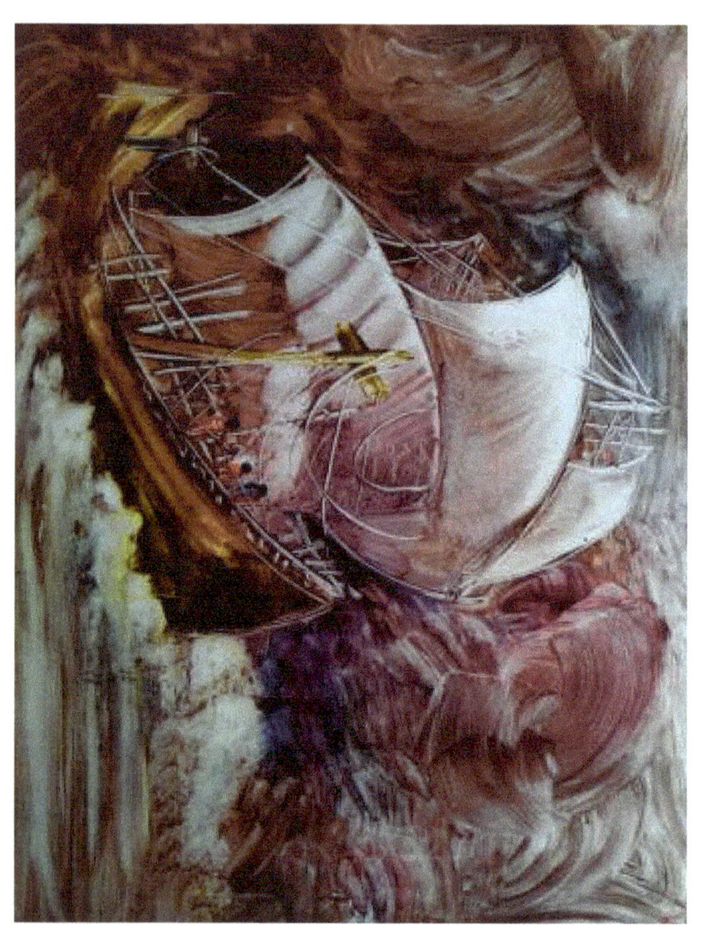

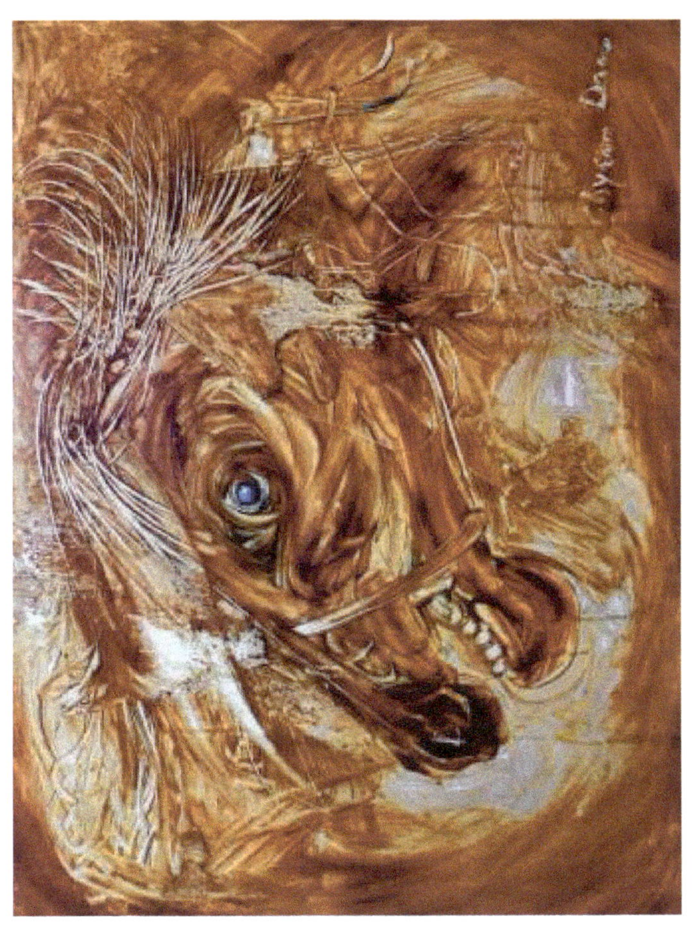

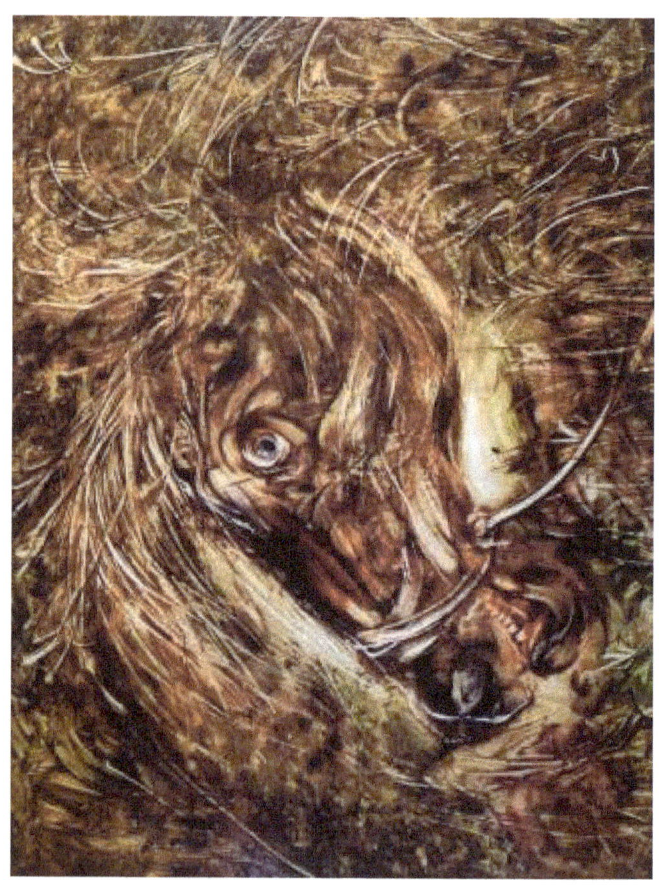

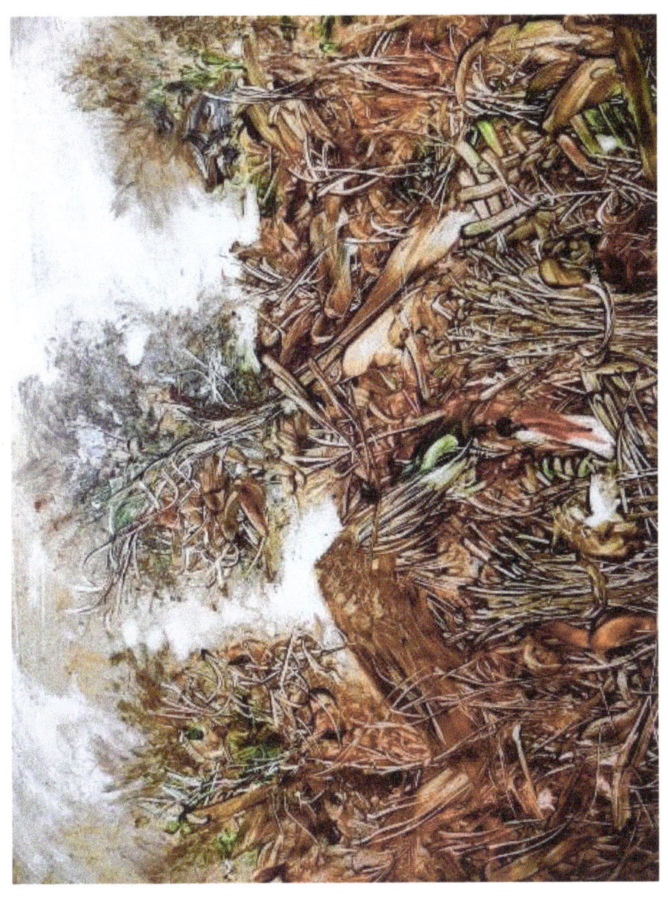

www.ingramcontent.com/pod-product-compliance
Ingram Content Group UK Ltd.
Pitfield, Milton Keynes, MK11 3LW, UK
UKHW062254290726
14090UKWH00017B/683

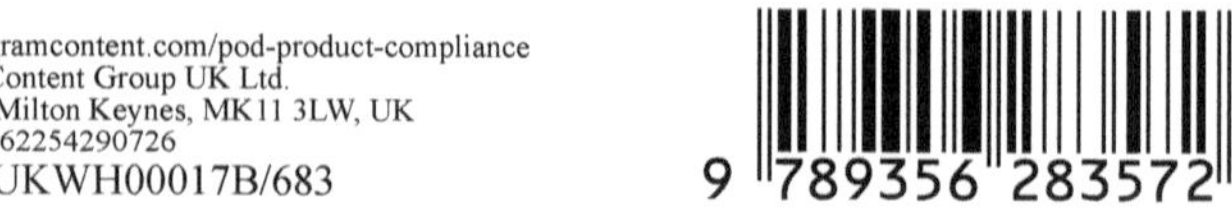

9 789356 283572